**International data
on anthropometry**

OCCUPATIONAL SAFETY
AND HEALTH SERIES
No. 65

INTERNATIONAL DATA ON ANTHROPOMETRY

Hans W. Jürgens
Ivar A. Aune
Ursula Pieper

English edition of the research report
Internationaler anthropometrischer Datenatlas,
published by the Federal Institute for
Occupational Safety and Health,
Dortmund, Federal Republic of Germany

INTERNATIONAL LABOUR OFFICE   GENEVA

ISBN 92-2-106449-2
ISSN 0078-3129

First published 1990

Printed by the International Labour Office, Geneva, Switzerland

Preface

There are great variations in the anthropometric measurements and body proportions of the world population. These anthropometric differences are reflected in the different standards that relate to each specific population. Increasing international economic interdependence, however, makes it necessary to go beyond national frontiers and to establish international anthropometric standards for consumer goods and the design of workplaces.

In this study the world population is classified in 20 groups according to measurement similarities. For each of these groups the 19 ergonomically important body measurements are compiled for both sexes for the percentiles 5, 50 and 95. As the ergonomic literature does not provide sufficient anthropometric data, additional information has been assembled from many other sources, and standardised and projected for the year 2000 on the basis of our present knowledge about the secular trend of acceleration.

In the final chapter an attempt is made to subdivide the world population into two different types according to body measurements and proportions. The resulting subdivision of the population into "northern people" and "southern people" is put forward as a new starting-point for the ergonomic design of consumer goods on a world-wide basis.

This English edition of the original document (Internationaler anthropometrischer Datenatlas) has been issued in co-operation with CIS, the International Safety and Health Information Centre of the ILO.

Table of contents

Page

1. Introduction

It has become generally recognised that both workplaces and products which are related to the human body must be designed with the body measurements and the range of movement of the people concerned in mind. In the Federal Republic of Germany and in many other countries this realisation has led to the adoption of standards adapted to the local population. As body measurements and proportions vary substantially from one another in different parts of the world, these national standards also vary considerably.

Internationally, the movement of people from one country to another is increasing and the volume of exported products is growing. Up until now, however, people have made do with products based on a more or less random mix of anthropometric data from various countries. The measurement tables constructed in this way differ in some cases quite considerably from the data for the Federal Republic of Germany. There has recently been a growing tendency to accept international standards as binding for the Federal Republic, and hence to lay down regulations affecting working conditions and products which diverge from the standards based on data appropriate to the local population. Regulations of this kind lead to hindrances and risks of accidents both at the workplace and for the consumer. They also handicap manufacturers in regard to both the internal market and exports.

Since the Federal Republic of Germany is increasingly affected by these developments because of the wide and complex nature of its international relations, we should not remain passive and be satisfied merely with piecemeal solutions to the obstacles and restrictions posed by inappropriate anthropometric measurements, but should rather take an active role with regard to emerging requirements.

In this monograph we therefore present what has so far been lacking: an international overview of ergonomically relevant body measurements and their distribution among populations so that an interested international readership may consider to what extent and in what way an international harmonisation of consumer goods and workplace design is necessary and possible.

2. An approach to the problem

The simplest way to solve the problem of standardising anthropometric data would have been for an international group of experts to establish the body measurements which are most important ergonomically, to compile them on a world-wide basis using a uniform method and to set out the results. However, this straightforward approach was excluded because of insurmountable organisational, technical and financial obstacles. There are already such great difficulties in putting together national anthropometric data on a representative basis that only a few countries have these figures available; in general, there are simply some data for limited groups, which are quite atypical of the population as a whole.

Since this straightforward approach to the problem was ruled out, it was necessary to fall back on a method based on evaluating available data. However, the fact that up to now there has been no comprehensive overview of ergonomically important body measurements on a world-wide basis highlights the difficulties of even this solution. Many individuals and institutions have indeed recorded body measurements in a number of regions, but these data are largely unrelated to ergonomic needs and are not comparable with one another. They cover vaguely defined sectors of the population; they are based on extremely different measurement procedures and thus lead to divergent results; and they also cover different periods of time. All these factors stand in the way of assembling comprehensive information for a world compilation.

In the light of all these points it was necessary to tackle the problem in six stages:

- assembly of all internationally available data from scientific and non-scientific literature and unpublished sources;

- obtaining additional information on the available data, such as measurement procedures, the bases of measurement and the sectors of population covered, so that the data could be compiled and made comparable;

- filling the gaps in the material from different surveys by extrapolation of missing data;

- standardisation of the results by relating them to a specified year; for planning reasons, this should be the year 2000;

- establishment of a world compilation; and

- classification of the available results with a view to an international harmonisation of consumer goods and workplaces.

The stages listed above, the assumptions made and the factors that exercise a significant influence are considered below.

3. The starting-point

During the early industrial period, in setting up environmental and working conditions for individuals and in manufacturing consumer goods, the mistake was frequently made of using mean values, i.e. the arithmetic mean of body measurements, as the basis for design.

The starting-point was thus a so-called "average person". The incorrectness of this procedure, which can still be met with today, has been referred to many times in the literature on ergonomics (cf., inter alia, Roebuck et al., 1975; Jürgens and Matzdorff, 1988). Since then account has been taken of the variety of measurements for people to be found in a population by classifying the available distribution of characteristics in percentiles and attempting to determine how the human environment can be adjusted to the different anthropometric groups of individuals. There are several different ways in which such an adaptation of objects to the human body can be made.

Adaptation. Those elements in the technical environment that are to be adapted to the human body are adjusted to the individual parts of the body by a provision for flexibility. Thus, for example, the height of a seat can be adjusted to the length of the lower leg, the depth of a seat to the length of the upper leg, the vertebral support, areas within reach, areas of vision, etc., by adjusting the dimensions to those of the part of the body directly concerned. This solution has the advantage that for each individual the variation of particular parts of the body from the anthropometric percentile can be taken into account (in so far as the adjustment facilities are not linked up with one another). A disadvantage of this solution of adaptation by adjustability lies in the fact that it becomes necessary to provide superfluous adjustment facilities in relation to the needs of the user population. An example of this would be: for motor vehicles to be sold in Scandinavia it would be an absurd waste of materials and an unnecessary addition to the vehicle's weight to provide them with adjustability arrangements so that they would be suitable for smaller individuals from South-East Asia to drive. The converse would apply in South-East Asia, where flexibility requirements to meet Scandinavians would never be used.

Differing "sizes". One possibility of adapting products to the varying body measurements and proportions of their users lies in producing goods in several different sizes, so that where these sizes are suitable and sufficiently numerous all the different combinations of measurements occurring in a population can be accommodated. This solution is used, for example, in the textile industry, for shoes and also for school seating. Its advantage lies in the fact that for each individual object there are no unnecessary adjustment provisions; the disadvantage is a logistical one, i.e. the need to hold sufficient stocks of all the different sizes and the fact that those items which are made to specific measurements, and cannot themselves be adjusted, are not available for use by persons with different measurements.

The critical measurement. If for organisational and technical reasons it is necessary to establish a single type of product for users of all body measurements (for example, steps, handrails in public areas, standard seats in public transport), reference should be made not to the average person, but rather to the appropriate "critical measurement", i.e. the design should take account of those groups of persons who determine the limits within which the item concerned is usable. For steps, for example, the vertical measurement should be established on the basis of the presumed upper limit for persons in the fifth body measurement percentile. For doors and passageways as well as bed lengths, the body measurements of the largest user represent the critical measurements. In designing seats, it is the users in the lower percentile range who must determine the measurements, as it is easier for a long-legged person to stretch out his or her legs than for a short-legged person to sit with the lower legs dangling.

Adjustment by selection of individuals. The most unsatisfactory solution, which should be avoided as far as possible on economic and social grounds lies in using an object of a fixed and unadjustable size, with the consequence that the person must fit the object or the workplace; this has the effect of preventing particular groups of people from making use of it. This situation may arise for purely physical reasons (astronauts, submarine crews, rowing coxes); but more often it arises from ignorance on the part of the manufacturer and has the result that large sectors of the population such as (frequently) women or older persons are hindered or prevented from using these products.

In the interest of human-oriented design of the working environment or whenever the need exists for a particularly good adaptation of external conditions to the individual, the choice should lie with adjustability or a range of different sizes, or a combination of both.

Experience at the national level has shown that almost all ergonomically important adaptation requirements (e.g. for longer-term use in the workplace) can be dealt with in this way. In many cases such adaptation has been made mandatory by legislative or regulatory authorities. In general, products can be adapted to persons with body measurements ranging from the

6   8582d

fifth to the 95th percentiles, even though at the two extremes difficulties - which can be remedied - will still occur.

Furthermore, since the national solutions now quite widely applied to problems of this nature in the Federal Republic of Germany and in some other European countries still meet with difficulties, it is safe to assume that any application of such national approaches at international level will also meet with difficulties.

Using the anthropometric data already available in this field as a starting-point, the attempt by the International Organization for Standardization (ISO) to develop a world-wide standard for earth-moving machinery based on the physical dimensions of operators (ISO 3411) has been especially noteworthy. Physical dimensions have been assembled on a world-wide basis and developed into an overall aggregate intended to determine the fifth and 95th percentile limits for the world population.

If we take as an example stature as an indicator (though only of limited use by itself): in the international standard we find a difference of 33 cm in height between the small operators (fifth percentile - P5) and the large ones (95th percentile - P95). This percentile difference in stature in the Federal Republic of Germany, by comparison, is about 21 cm, if we only look at one sex. However, if we apply the percentile limits to both sexes, there is a difference of 33 cm between P5 women and P95 men. It so happens, then, that body measurements from the Federal Republic of Germany correspond, by and large, to those of the ISO for earth-moving machinery operators. If we consider other countries, however, we find values for P95 men in northern Europe and in the United States which are 50 mm over the P95 ISO value. On the other hand, we see that in southern Europe, and even more so outside Europe, the values for women are far below the P5 value for the earth-moving machinery operator. The workstation dimensions determined by the ISO thus exclude most of the female population of the world, which appears unacceptable (Matzdorff, 1987).

It is important to determine appropriate anthropometric dimensions not only from the standpoint of social and labour market policy but also for economic reasons. This becomes particularly necessary if mass-produced goods related to the human body are marketed internationally. If a large proportion of the population is not able to use these goods, this can also adversely affect market prospects.

A particular problem arises from the fact that, given a lack of international standards on body dimensions, both manufacturers and consumers of some products tend to develop specific standards for particular products. Thus, in addition to the standard for earth-moving machinery operators, an anthropometric standard for tractor operators has also been drawn up (ISO 3789), and there is a real risk that other specific patterns of human dimensions for particular products will be developed and that, like their forerunners, they will be based on inadequate data.

This trend could result in a confusing and conflicting multiplicity of standards, which would fail to provide either the users of these goods or their manufacturers and distributors with the support that should be expected from standardisation.

Meanwhile, it has become recognised that international determination of physical dimensions requires a systematic anthropometric coverage of all the relevant populations. This should be based on representativeness in the sense that both sexes, all age groups that are actively at work, all economic and social sectors, all regional and race differences and also the secular trend of acceleration must be taken into account.

It is only on the basis of such knowledge that one can make appropriate decisions in relation to adapting the human environment to the population and decide on adjustability, groups of sizes, critical measurements and their combinations.

4. Evaluation of existing material

For a long time measurements have been taken of the human body, with different purposes and ideas in mind. A comparatively small proportion of them have been body measurements for ergonomic purposes, since it is only relatively recently that importance has been attached to designing workplaces and products to fit human beings. Even though the body dimensions available in the literature and from other sources were not assembled for economic purposes, they can lead to important ergonomic and anthropometric conclusions provided that they are appropriately processed and completed; and in view of the lack of ergonomic anthropometrical data these non-ergonomic data provide an important information base for ergonomists as well.

The first step was to check what data sources were available, and in particular for what specific purposes. The following were of special practical importance:

- Anthropometric measurements made by handicraft workers. This is basically the measurement of an individual's physical dimensions with the aim of adapting consumer goods. This was a practice in general use in the pre-industrial era, but it is also in existence today in some areas. It provides a whole volume of physical measurement data which can be deduced from the measurement books of tailors, shoemakers, and to some extent carpenters, orthopaedic and dental technicians, and others. The direct relationship to an individual means that such data are naturally not representative of a whole population; nevertheless, when they are assembled and standardised with the aid of comparative values for the population, these individual anthropometric data do provide the basis for further calculation and evaluation.

- Anthropological anthropometrics. By far the greatest volume, and internationally by far the most important range of information, is that derived from anthropological research. This consists of investigations of populations rather than studies of individuals. The measurement points and the procedures are mostly well documented, so that it is possible to make further use of the measurements. In addition, the regional and racial distributions, as well as social and economic differences, are generally known. The disadvantage of these anthropometric data, however, lies in the fact that the measurements were not taken in order to apply them to the design of the human environment, but were rather in the form of basic attempts to define groups, determine differences and produce classifications. Thus, in many cases the measurements taken (e.g. numerous head measurements) were originally of marginal interest to ergonomics. However, the proportional relationships and frameworks relating to the entire body obtained in this context provide an important basis on which data of ergonomic value can be extrapolated. Efforts to rework these anthropological measurements into ergonomically valid data were already undertaken in 1960 (Jürgens, 1960).

- Medical anthropometrics. As any detailed medical examination includes the recording of some body measurements, comprehensive data are obtainable from medical documentation and patient case histories. The restriction of these data to a few items such as stature, chest measurement and body weight, plus in some cases wrist size and a few others, naturally imposes a considerable limitation on their ergonomic value. However, the world-wide extent of data collection of this kind at least provides guidance on variations in measurements between different populations. In the field of medical anthropometrics, particular interest is attached to the measurements from orthopaedic clinics and anatomical and pathological institutions, which in many cases are very detailed, and also to measurements in the context of medical examinations for insurance and those taken by public health workers. These involved, inter alia, physical dimensions and proportions in relation to body posture and development, and were used in early ergonomic studies (e.g. in the design of school seats).

- Sport anthropometrics. There has been a long tradition of anthropometric investigation of athletes, as attempts have constantly been made to relate athletic performance to body dimensions and proportions. For example, for some decades the Olympic Games have been accompanied by anthropometric investigations in which detailed measurements were made of persons from populations in all parts of the world. A special area of sport anthropometrics, which has recently been growing in importance, is that of determining suitability of body dimensions for particular types of sport. A major disadvantage of the data from sport anthropometrics is that they cover an atypical population specially selected for its particular physical abilities, which is also unrepresentative in terms of age composition. The results of investigations by sport anthropometrists, when viewed from an ergonomic standpoint, should therefore be evaluated particularly carefully, having regard to their inherent regional and race differences.

- <u>Investigations of growth</u>. Many studies dealing with human growth and development have been constructed largely on the basis of anthropometric records. Such data are thus available for a number of different populations throughout the world. Such studies have, however, the disadvantage, from the ergonomic point of view, that, with the exception of those concentrating on special questions of environmental design for children and young people, it is only the end group in these growth surveys that is identical with the starting group and who, as adults, are substantial users of ergonomic designs.

- <u>Forensic anthropometrics</u>. A limited field, which nevertheless can provide some valuable data for extrapolation, is that of investigations carried out in the context of legal proceedings. These are measurement studies for the identification of individuals, and data from morphological expert opinions on paternity cases, which are very numerous in some countries, and which are generally accompanied by comprehensive anthropometric statistics.

- <u>Ergonomic anthropometrics</u>. The field of ergonomic anthropometrics itself, in spite of its recognised practical importance, has only recently been explored intensively and on a broad basis. The ergonomic objective of most of the studies hitherto available in the literature has not been a world-wide one: indeed it has frequently not even covered the whole of a single country's environmental and production design problems but has instead been restricted to limited social and regional populations.

   Of special importance here are the examinations of military service personnel, as in this area there has for decades been a need for particularly appropriate adaptation of equipment and environment to the physical form and functions of the user. In addition, it is especially easy from the organisational standpoint to have access to military service personnel for examination.

   Alongside these anthropometric examinations of military service personnel, which are numerically very important world-wide, there are studies specific to individual products, undertaken by or at the request of manufacturers' and consumers' organisations, and to some extent also by safety and insurance experts. A variety of anthropometric investigations have been carried out, particularly in the textile industry, shoe manufacture, office equipment, motor vehicle production, and in relation to safety at work.

When classifying the available data by regions, we may observe that European populations, in particular those of the highly industrialised countries, have already been well researched anthropometrically. Outside Europe, large quantities of data are available in particular for the United States, as well as voluminous records of examinations carried out by the United States in relation to military service personnel of other countries, e.g. in the Mediterranean, and in East and South-East Asia. Substantial independent anthropometric results are also available from India and Japan. Ergonomic anthropometric investigations are being carried out on a national scale in China at the present time.

A general problem of all these investigations, however, is that either individually or as a whole they indicate differences between single individuals and between populations or sections of the population, but do not take into account the effect on body measurements of the secular trend of acceleration. Taking stature as an indicator, we can observe that during the last 100 years in the countries where this trend is most in evidence it has resulted in an average increase in height of over 14 cm; until two decades ago the increase was 1 cm per decade, but more recently this rate of increase has doubled and - for example in the Federal Republic of Germany - has reflected increases of over 2 cm per decade. The world's populations are affected very differently from one another by this trend, which is not constant. Some populations are not yet affected and others are no longer affected. But overall and over a long period of time it does reflect an ergonomically significant change in physical dimensions. These developments are known but have not yet been systematically embodied in ergonomic evaluations of body dimensions (cf. Roebuck et al., 1975).

A second and different problem is the question of the representativeness of the available sample surveys. It has long been known that women's physical dimensions and proportions are different from those of men and it is also known that younger people can be clearly distinguished from older persons, not only because of the different ways in which they are affected by the acceleration process, but also because of age-related changes in physical dimensions. It has also been established in detail by numerous anthropological anthropometric investigations how and in what ways populations in different regions and of different races vary in their physical dimensions and proportions. And finally, many studies have also determined that differences in physical dimensions related to occupational and social group are of ergonomic importance.

This multiplicity of differentiating factors means that in making an ergonomic evaluation of anthropometric data it is necessary to check comparability and to achieve standardisation of the results so as to make them representative of the entire population (or that part of it being considered). In this respect, there are still many shortcomings with regard to data integrity, and mistakes, which could easily be avoided, are still being repeated.

Another important point is the extent to which physical dimensions can be represented and compared. The complicated morphology of the human body means that it is not at all easy to determine how a given dimension (e.g. the length of a limb) is to be measured. Depending on the choice of measurement points and methods, and on the body postures of the persons being measured and measuring respectively, there are considerable differences, which are ergonomically relevant. During the last 100 years many efforts have been made to achieve international uniformity in methods of measurement. These efforts have led to a certain degree of world-wide agreement, at least in the narrower field of anthropology and ergonomics. However, even among qualified anthropometric researchers there are differences of method and concept, quite apart from measuring errors, which can lead to substantial variations in the results, depending on the difficulty of the measurement being made, and on the training of the person carrying it out (Lewin and Jürgens, 1969).

Even if one refrains from making assertions as to the representativeness of physical dimensions, the very fact of having to document and compare measurement points and procedures in research on physical dimensions means that numerous studies, which were not specially prepared, must be disregarded because they are not comparable and, therefore, cannot be used for ergonomic purposes. Thus Krogman (1941) reported that out of 600 studies on growth anthropometrics he had been unable to use almost half because of inadequate data on measurement points and methods which would have permitted proper comparisons. Garrett and Kennedy (1971) attempted an international survey of ergonomically usable and significant body measurements world-wide in an analysis which is outstanding for its precision and thoroughness. They found only 39 studies which were sufficiently documented to be usable as sources for ergonomic anthropometrics without further work being done on them. In this connection, the authors analysed 2,000 descriptions of anthropometric data in detail.

The problems outlined above clearly indicate the limitations associated with the establishment of an ergonomic anthropometric data bank. The limited comparability of data, the problems of representativeness and the varying extent to which different populations form part of the secular trend of acceleration make it practically impossible to summarise or to subdivide and classify the data available from the literature. Thus, an ergonomic anthropometric data bank can in practice be only a bibliographical assembly of individual investigations with information on their contents. There is no clear way in which the data can be merged.

This review of the data sources, their regional distribution, the times at which they were collected and their significance make it clear that any conclusions put forward on ergonomically significant anthropometric data of the world population may be based on information from all parts of the world covering numerous different populations and groups of population. However, in terms of representativeness, measurement points and methods, the number of measurements covered and their statistical treatment, this information displays great lack of uniformity and would need substantial reworking to make it comparable.

One way of dealing with the problems and risks described here could be along the following lines:

- the whole population of the world could be subdivided into groups on the basis of measurement similarities;

- this subdivision by groups could then be supplemented by a subdivision based on regional factors in order to determine the anthropometrically important proportions typical of different ethnic groups;

- these groups would include only populations which are sufficiently numerous to fall between the fifth and 95th percentiles of the world population (so that numerically small populations with extreme body measurements such as the African pygmies or the Nilotes would be left out);

- gaps in the data occurring for some body measurements in the individual groups would be interpolated by computer from the existing pattern of proportions with the help of indicative measurements; and

- all the investigations would be recalculated to bring them to a uniform position in time, taking into account the known and foreseeable participation in the secular trend of acceleration.

The result of the data treated in this way would be an anthropometric world compilation which would provide, for each of the groups covered, a complete set of the most important body measurements distributed over the fifth, 50th and 95th percentiles for both sexes and projected uniformly to the year 2000.

5. Methods

5.1 The sources available and those actually used

The data sources needed for the present investigation were acquired over a 30-year period from the authors' anthropometric investigation in all parts of the world and from the national and international activities related to standardisation in this field. In addition, the ten-year period of preparation for this specific investigation has made possible an intensive effort to obtain not only the generally available sources documented in the bibliography at the end of this monograph covering the fields of work referred to in Chapter 4, but also an evaluation of the so-called "grey" literature and unpublished data, some of which (as in Poland and Italy) were obtained by specific visits to institutions active in the anthropometric field. Furthermore, many items of body measurement data related to specific products in industry were evaluated.

In order to limit the effects of the secular trend of acceleration (see section 5.7, below), of migrations and of other demographic changes on the morphology of the populations concerned, information was taken almost exclusively from anthropometric investigations carried out after 1960. The exception was the studies used for establishing and measuring the secular trend of acceleration.

5.2 The choice of measurements for the world compilation

The number of possible measurement points and measurement ranges is almost unlimited. In the anthropological anthropometric literature several thousands of these have been documented. From the ergonomic viewpoint this figure can be reduced substantially, as in this context anthropometrics are not required to produce as comprehensive as possible a description of people, but rather to determine the interaction between people and their environment within the framework of specific technical requirements. The elements which mainly concern us here are the arm reach and leg movement areas, the field of vision, the trunk, and measurements required for adapting some objects which are directly next to the body.

The measurement programme limited in this way can be broken down into three sections based on existing correlations:

- the height-length measurements of the body which have a positive correlation of between 0.6 and 0.9;

- the width-depth-girth-weight measurements which have a positive correlation of up to 0.6; and finally

- the two measurement subgroups relating to the head and the hands.

The relationships of these sections to one another are comparatively loose. For the compilation, however, it will be necessary to characterise each of the measurement groups mentioned above by examples illustrating the correlative relationships of more or less independent groups, in order in particular to clarify the varying importance of these measurements for sex, age and race differentiation. At the same time, it is possible, starting from measurements in a particular area (e.g. the height-length measurements), to obtain other measurements from the same cluster on the basis of existing correlations.

The selection and delimitation of the measurements to be used for the anthropometric world compilation were derived from the above considerations, which are also in line with the proposals of other researchers to such an extent that selection of the internationally available body measurements was primarily limited to the field we are referring to here.

A particular point should be considered when using the measurement of stature. Stature is traditionally and world-wide by far the most frequently recorded measurement, but ergonomically it is of direct importance only for very limited areas such as passageways and beds. Stature is used primarily as an indicative measurement, with the implicit assumption that a person of tall stature will also be above the average value in his or her other body measurements. But this assumption is true only to a limited extent. There are, of course, relatively high correlations between stature and the various measurements of body length, but the relationships between stature and width, depth, girth and weight are relatively less significant. Thus, for example, the correlation between stature and chest measurement is 0.13. Stature is therefore unsuitable as a universal indicative measurement. However, within the area of length measurements itself there are a number of characteristic differences for different groups of measurements. Thus the ratio of trunk measurements to stature, for instance, is invariably greater for women than for men. In this respect there are also clear racial differences as the ratio of trunk to stature is noticeably lower for Negroids and Europeans than for Mongolians. These facts indicate that the use of stature as an indicator requires at the very least that specific distinctions be drawn on the basis of sex and race.

For measurements of width, depth and girth, in order to avoid short-term fluctuations due to dietary factors and other conditions, it would be most appropriate to rely on a skeletal width measurement, such as the shoulder width measured as acromial width.

5.3 Standardisation of methods of measurement

As the experience of Krogman (1941) and Garrett and Kennedy (1971) has shown, most of the studies available in the literature on methods of measurement and definitions of these measurements are inadequate or not documented at all. This means that if we are to make use of these results, it is essential to have information on the methods of measurement used. Even though the measurements are not individually defined, it is to some exent possible, using the literature on methods referred to in the bibliography (e.g. the internationally used standard work of Rudolf Martin, 1914, 1928, 1957-66, 1988), to make deductions as to the methods used. It is also possible to draw some conclusions from the work of living authors by means of personal contacts and from the work of authors no longer living by consulting anthropometric teaching staff. In the meantime, one cannot make use of all the available measurements, which have not been defined uniformly, but can simply deduce proportional relationships.

5.4 Different measurements for the sexes

As a general rule, all the populations to be covered in the world compilation should be differentiated by sex. The data on body measurements of women are much scarcer in the ergonomic anthropometric literature than those of men. But because of the increasing participation of women in all types of work and also on account of their role as consumers of everyday products, there is an even greater need for measurements of women than for those of men. Therefore, the gaps in the ergonomic anthropometric literature have been substantially filled on a standard basis by the much more comprehensive anthropological anthropometric literature and by data from medical anthropometrics.

5.5 Choice of age group for the world compilation

The values incorporated in the compilation concern the age group 25-45 years. Two considerations were of primary importance in selecting this age group. On the one hand, by far the greatest proportion of available data, including from the industrialised countries, is restricted to this age group; on the other, this age group covers those persons who have completed their period of growth and are, to some extent, in a stationary phase of metrical development. The period after the age of 45 produces increasing changes in the body shape due to involution processes.

5.6 Extrapolation of missing anthropometric data

As the lack of anthropometric data for ergonomic studies has regularly been a problem, consideration was given to this at an early stage and procedures were developed for deducing unavailable values from those available (Barkla, 1961). More comprehensive methodical approaches are given by Roebuck et al. (1975) and Pheasant (1982). Further guide-lines for a data completion process going beyond racial distinctions are to be found in Pheasant (1986). There has also been a systematic investigation (Jürgens, 1984) of the possibilities of error that arise in the case of such data extrapolation procedures. One can therefore say that these procedures are today acceptable in practice. There is also a special provision for correction of the effects of the secular trend of acceleration.

5.7 Projection of the secular trend of acceleration

There are few phenomena in modern human biology which have been so thoroughly investigated, but whose causes and development have been so inadequately explained, as the secular trend of acceleration. Since the second half of the last century, this trend has been reflected in changes in the biological growth and maturing processes, which constitute the total phenomenon of acceleration but which are in no way uniform, static or following a consistent pattern of fluctuation. For ergonomic and anthropometric questions, it is basically only the metrical data affecting adults that are of concern.

It is, however, by no means a simple matter to assemble data on these changes and their differences over a period of time or to examine them from the ergonomic standpoint, as the anthropometric assessment of the acceleration process is generally based on the stature of fully grown individuals. To a very considerable extent, however, growth investigations on schoolchildren and students and recruitment examinations for military service have been used. The change over time of the average measurements thus obtained is termed "acceleration".

A procedure based on this assumption depends on the fulfilment of certain conditions which are generally not sufficiently taken into account:

- The very great majority of all the investigations of the acceleration problem described in the literature use measurements of the type of origin described above, on the assumption that these are values representing the end of the growth process. On this assumption, 18-20 year-olds have reached their full stature. This is, in fact, not at all the case (Büchi, 1950; Miall et al., 1967; Jürgens, 1968), as half of all the men surveyed continued to show growth up to the age of 30 years. For this reason, measurement of the acceleration process with the aid of investigations of schoolchildren or military recruits does not give the ergonomically important final values.

- In many populations there is a social differentiation of the increase in stature due to acceleration. Backwin and McLaughlin (1964) were able to demonstrate that persons from the upper social strata no longer show an increase in stature due to the secular trend of acceleration, in sharp contrast to those from the lower strata. A similar result was obtained for the population of the Federal Republic of Germany (Jürgens, 1966).

- In the literature there is frequently confusion between group differences in stature and changes due to acceleration. It has been known for centuries that in many places the body measurements of urban populations are greater than those of rural populations. The same applies to upper social strata in comparison with lower ones. One should, however, not conclude that one group is accelerating faster than the other. The groups are different, but as long as no sequential data are available on body measurement trends in the population, it remains an open question whether differences are due to a varying degree of participation in the acceleration trend or whether they arise for other reasons.

- The secular trend of acceleration is not constant, but rather has periods of time without any movement - sometimes for specific groups, sometimes for the whole population of a country. In one or two cases, there have even been reports of diminution in stature (Kenntner, 1963; Roche, 1979). In the Federal Republic of Germany, however, the acceleration has increased during the last 20 years.

The cause of the secular trend of acceleration is unknown. One assumes the combined effect of a series of influencing factors. For most of these factors it is assumed that they cannot all be operating freely in the same direction and with the same effect, but that one is faced with a drop in the acceleration until a "saturation point" is reached (Jürgens, 1961; Schneider et al., 1983; Pheasant, 1986). This assumption corresponds to the present state of knowledge but no firm confirmation has been established owing to the fact that the causes of acceleration are not yet known.

An acceleration trend is at present in evidence for all the industrialised countries of the world. It can, however, also be assumed to apply to parts of the population in the non-industrialised countries. This is particularly true for many countries in Central and South America as well as in Asia, especially South-East Asia (Kogi and Sen, 1987). Based on the hypotheses referred to above as to the continuing process of acceleration in the industrialised countries, we have based our main calculations on the premise that the present increase in stature will have ceased by the year 2000, the date taken as a yardstick for this investigation. For countries in which a beginning of the acceleration has been noted among parts of the population, we have taken this into account when extrapolating the acceleration trend up to the year 2000. Those countries in which there has so far been no indication of an acceleration trend have been regarded as static from this stand-point up to the year 2000.

The anthropometric aspect of acceleration is generally deduced from the indicative measurement of stature. As already explained, this measurement is of secondary importance ergonomically. Much more important are the trunk and extremity measurements. The question therefore arises as to how these change in relation to stature during the course of the acceleration trend.

A series of investigations (Jürgens, 1960; Borkan et al., 1983; Pheasant, 1986) have clearly shown that during the process of acceleration there is no shift in the proportions, i.e. that the human body grows equally during the secular trend of acceleration. However the Japanese population provides an exception to this world-wide regularity (Tanner et al., 1982; Ohyama et al., 1987). Here, there is a reported increase in the leg/body height ratio. This exception has to be taken into account in the overall calculation of data for the Japanese population projected to the year 2000. One notes in general that no differences between the sexes arise during the course of the acceleration process.

6. International anthropometric and ergonomic compilation

The compilation incorporates 19 ergonomically important body measurements which are appropriate as indicative measurements for further anthropometric constructions. For each measurement the percentiles five, 50 and 95 are given in each case for both men and women. The definitions of body measurement are those given in DIN 33402, Part 1 and, for those measurements not included, those given in Handbook of ergonomics (BWB, 1979-88).

A special explanation and justification is needed for the regional breakdown of the body measurement tables into 20 populations. As mentioned previously, the following factors were considered significant in relation to the regional breakdown used here:

- biological, i.e. mainly racial uniformity, to the extent that this can be determined anthropometrically;

- numerical (demographic) importance of the populations;

- a breakdown by countries has been applied only where there is general conformity with the biological breakdown. It was frequently necessary to put several countries together, while others, whose populations are not sufficiently uniform, were broken down into distinct units.

On the basis of the above principles, the world population was broken down into the following regions:

1. North America
2. Latin America (Indian pop.)
3. L. America (Europ.-negroid pop.)
4. Northern Europe
5. Central Europe
6. Eastern Europe
7. South-eastern Europe
8. France
9. Iberian Peninsula
10. North Africa
11. West Africa
12. South-eastern Africa
13. Near East
14. North India
15. South India
16. North Asia
17. South China
18. South-East Asia
19. Australia (European pop.)
20. Japan

Body measurement tables (in millimetres) for these 20 regions follow, together with explanatory sheets describing the literature used as the basis for the tables.

Body measurements for Region 1 (North America)

Measurement	Men			Women			Min.	Max.
Percentile:	5	50	95	5	50	95		
Stature	1 670	1 790	1 900	1 540	1 650	1 760	1 540	1 900
Sitting height	890	930	990	820	880	930	820	990
Eye height, sitting	760	810	860	700	760	810	700	860
Forward reach (fingertips)	790	850	910	730	800	870	730	910
Shoulder breadth (bideltoid)	420	460	500	370	400	430	370	500
Shoulder breadth (biacromial)	365	395	430	330	360	385	330	430
Hip breadth (standing)	305	340	365	310	350	405	305	405
Knee height	505	550	600	460	500	550	460	600
Lower leg length (popliteal height)	405	445	500	360	410	450	360	500
Elbow-grip length	325	360	385	295	330	355	295	385
Buttock-knee length	550	600	660	520	570	630	520	660
Buttock-heel length	990	1 080	1 180	940	1 030	1 130	940	1 180
Hip breadth (sitting)	310	350	400	310	370	430	310	430
Hand length	175	190	205	160	170	190	160	205
Hand breadth	80	85	90	70	75	85	70	90
Foot length	250	265	285	220	245	260	220	285
Head circumference	550	575	600	520	545	575	520	600
Head length	185	195	205	165	180	195	165	205
Head breadth	145	155	165	135	145	155	135	165

Body measurements for Region 2 (Latin America – Indian population)

Measurement	Men			Women			Min.	Max.
Percentile:	5	50	95	5	50	95		
Stature	1 520	1 620	1 710	1 390	1 480	1 560	1 390	1 710
Sitting height	810	850	900	760	800	840	760	900
Eye height, sitting	720	760	800	660	700	740	660	800
Forward reach (fingertips)	730	780	820	670	710	750	670	820
Shoulder breadth (bideltoid)	400	430	460	360	380	410	360	460
Shoulder breadth (biacromial)	350	370	395	330	355	370	330	395
Hip breadth (standing)	260	280	320	270	290	330	260	330
Knee height	465	495	520	405	445	485	405	520
Lower leg length (popliteal height)	365	390	410	320	360	390	320	410
Elbow-grip length	295	325	360	270	295	325	270	360
Buttock-knee length	500	530	560	450	485	510	450	560
Buttock-heel length	900	980	1 050	830	910	990	830	1 050
Hip breadth (sitting)	260	290	340	270	310	355	260	355
Hand length	165	180	195	150	165	175	150	195
Hand breadth	75	80	85	65	70	75	65	85
Foot length	230	245	270	210	230	245	210	270
Head circumference	520	540	560	495	515	530	495	560
Head length	175	185	190	165	175	185	165	190
Head breadth	145	150	155	135	145	150	135	155

Body measurements for Region 3 (Latin America - European and Negroid population)

Measurement	Men			Women				
Percentile:	5	50	95	5	50	95	Min.	Max.
Stature	1 650	1 750	1 850	1 520	1 620	1 720	1 520	1 850
Sitting height	870	930	990	810	860	920	810	990
Eye height, sitting	750	810	870	700	760	820	700	870
Forward reach (fingertips)	790	840	890	710	780	830	710	890
Shoulder breadth (bideltoid)	420	450	490	370	400	430	370	490
Shoulder breadth (biacromial)	360	400	430	320	350	390	320	430
Hip breadth (standing)	310	340	375	315	350	405	310	405
Knee height	500	540	560	435	480	540	435	560
Lower leg length (popliteal height)	405	445	480	340	380	440	340	480
Elbow-grip length	320	350	390	290	325	360	290	390
Buttock-knee length	540	580	620	510	540	580	510	620
Buttock-heel length	970	1 050	1 130	920	990	1 070	920	1 130
Hip breadth (sitting)	320	350	395	320	365	430	320	430
Hand length	170	180	195	155	165	175	155	195
Hand breadth	80	85	90	65	70	80	65	90
Foot length	240	260	285	215	240	265	215	285
Head circumference	535	565	595	515	540	565	515	595
Head length	180	190	205	170	175	190	170	205
Head breadth	150	155	165	140	150	160	140	165

Body measurements for Region 4 (Northern Europe)

Measurement	Men			Women				
Percentile:	5	50	95	5	50	95	Min.	Max.
Stature	1 710	1 810	1 910	1 580	1 690	1 790	1 580	1 910
Sitting height	900	950	1 000	840	900	950	840	1 000
Eye height, sitting	770	820	870	710	760	820	710	870
Forward reach (fingertips)	820	870	930	740	810	870	740	930
Shoulder breadth (bideltoid)	425	460	500	365	400	430	365	500
Shoulder breadth (biacromial)	360	400	430	320	355	385	320	430
Hip breadth (standing)	310	340	370	315	350	405	310	405
Knee height	505	550	600	460	500	550	460	600
Lower leg length (popliteal height)	415	455	505	370	410	450	370	505
Elbow-grip length	330	370	400	310	335	370	310	400
Buttock-knee length	580	630	670	540	590	630	540	670
Buttock-heel length	1 000	1 100	1 190	960	1 050	1 130	960	1 190
Hip breadth (sitting)	320	350	390	325	375	430	320	430
Hand length	185	195	205	160	175	195	160	205
Hand breadth	80	90	95	70	80	85	70	95
Foot length	240	260	280	230	250	275	230	280
Head circumference	550	580	600	520	550	580	520	600
Head length	185	195	205	170	180	195	170	205
Head breadth	145	155	170	140	150	160	140	170

Body measurements for Region 5 (Central Europe)

Measurement	Men			Women			Min.	Max.
Percentile:	5	50	95	5	50	95		
Stature	1 670	1 770	1 860	1 550	1 660	1 750	1 550	1 860
Sitting height	880	940	980	820	880	930	820	980
Eye height, sitting	740	800	850	700	750	810	700	850
Forward reach (fingertips)	800	850	890	740	800	840	740	890
Shoulder breadth (bideltoid)	420	460	490	365	420	455	365	490
Shoulder breadth (biacromial)	365	400	430	340	365	405	340	430
Hip breadth (standing)	310	350	375	315	360	410	310	410
Knee height	495	550	595	460	500	540	460	595
Lower leg length (popliteal height)	420	465	500	390	425	460	390	500
Elbow-grip length	330	360	390	300	325	370	300	390
Buttock-knee length	550	610	660	530	580	630	530	660
Buttock-heel length	985	1 070	1 150	930	1 000	1 080	930	1 150
Hip breadth (sitting)	310	365	390	330	400	440	310	440
Hand length	175	190	205	160	175	190	160	205
Hand breadth	80	90	95	70	75	85	70	95
Foot length	240	265	285	220	240	260	220	285
Head circumference	540	575	600	520	550	590	520	600
Head length	180	190	200	170	180	190	170	200
Head breadth	145	155	165	135	145	155	135	165

8582d

Body measurements for Region 6 (Eastern Europe)

Measurement	Men			Women			Min.	Max.
Percentile:	5	50	95	5	50	95		
Stature	1 660	1 750	1 850	1 540	1 630	1 720	1 540	1 850
Sitting height	860	910	960	830	870	910	830	960
Eye height, sitting	730	790	850	670	730	790	670	850
Forward reach (fingertips)	800	840	890	740	780	820	740	890
Shoulder breadth (bideltoid)	410	450	490	370	410	450	370	490
Shoulder breadth (biacromial)	350	390	420	320	355	380	320	420
Hip breadth (standing)	305	345	385	315	360	405	305	405
Knee height	490	550	590	445	510	540	445	590
Lower leg length (popliteal height)	395	445	490	375	405	430	375	490
Elbow-grip length	325	350	390	300	325	360	300	390
Buttock-knee length	550	600	650	520	570	610	520	650
Buttock-heel length	990	1 070	1 150	930	1 010	1 090	930	1 150
Hip breadth (sitting)	310	360	400	325	380	435	310	435
Hand length	175	190	205	155	175	190	155	205
Hand breadth	80	90	100	75	80	85	75	100
Foot length	245	265	285	225	245	265	225	285
Head circumference	540	570	600	530	550	580	530	600
Head length	180	190	200	170	180	190	170	200
Head breadth	150	155	165	145	150	160	145	165

8582d

Body measurements for Region 7 (South-eastern Europe)

Measurement	Men			Women			Min.	Max.
Percentile:	5	50	95	5	50	95		
Stature	1 640	1 730	1 830	1 530	1 620	1 720	1 530	1 830
Sitting height	860	900	960	800	860	900	800	960
Eye height, sitting	740	790	840	680	730	780	680	840
Forward reach (fingertips)	790	830	880	740	780	830	740	880
Shoulder breadth (bideltoid)	420	450	490	365	405	430	365	490
Shoulder breadth (biacromial)	360	395	430	320	350	390	320	430
Hip breadth (standing)	310	340	370	315	350	400	310	400
Knee height	490	535	580	425	460	495	425	580
Lower leg length (popliteal height)	410	455	485	340	380	420	340	485
Elbow-grip length	320	345	385	300	325	360	300	385
Buttock-knee length	570	600	650	530	570	610	530	650
Buttock-heel length	970	1 040	1 110	920	1 000	1 080	920	1 110
Hip breadth (sitting)	310	355	390	320	370	430	310	430
Hand length	175	190	205	160	175	190	160	205
Hand breadth	80	90	95	70	75	85	70	95
Foot length	245	265	285	220	240	260	220	285
Head circumference	550	570	590	530	550	570	530	590
Head length	175	190	205	160	175	190	160	205
Head breadth	145	155	165	140	150	160	140	165

Body measurements for Region 8 (France)

Measurement	Men			Women				
Percentile:	5	50	95	5	50	95	Min.	Max.
Stature	1 660	1 770	1 890	1 530	1 630	1 740	1 530	1 890
Sitting height	870	930	980	820	860	910	820	980
Eye height, sitting	750	800	850	690	730	780	690	850
Forward reach (fingertips)	800	850	910	730	780	830	730	910
Shoulder breadth (bideltoid)	410	450	490	370	410	430	370	490
Shoulder breadth (biacromial)	360	390	420	320	350	390	320	420
Hip breadth (standing)	310	340	370	315	350	400	310	400
Knee height	495	540	580	455	490	525	455	580
Lower leg length (popliteal height)	390	445	490	345	385	425	345	490
Elbow-grip length	325	355	395	300	325	365	300	395
Buttock-knee length	560	620	660	520	570	610	520	660
Buttock-heel length	990	1 060	1 130	920	990	1 070	920	1 130
Hip breadth (sitting)	315	350	380	320	375	430	315	430
Hand length	180	195	210	160	170	180	160	210
Hand breadth	80	90	95	70	75	85	70	95
Foot length	245	265	285	220	235	255	220	285
Head circumference	540	570	600	520	550	570	520	600
Head length	180	195	205	170	180	190	170	205
Head breadth	145	155	165	135	140	150	135	165

8582d

Body measurements for Region 9 (Iberian Peninsula)

Measurement	Men			Women			Min.	Max.
Percentile:	5	50	95	5	50	95		
Stature	1 580	1 710	1 830	1 510	1 600	1 700	1 510	1 830
Sitting height	830	890	950	800	850	900	800	950
Eye height, sitting	720	790	850	680	740	810	680	850
Forward reach (fingertips)	760	820	880	720	770	820	720	880
Shoulder breadth (bideltoid)	400	440	480	350	390	430	350	480
Shoulder breadth (biacromial)	340	380	420	310	350	390	310	420
Hip breadth (standing)	295	340	370	300	350	400	295	400
Knee height	470	520	570	445	480	520	445	570
Lower leg length (popliteal height)	400	440	480	340	380	420	340	480
Elbow-grip length	310	340	385	295	320	360	295	385
Buttock-knee length	540	590	640	510	560	600	510	640
Buttock-heel length	950	1 030	1 100	890	940	1 000	890	1 100
Hip breadth (sitting)	300	345	390	310	360	425	300	425
Hand length	170	185	215	155	175	200	155	215
Hand breadth	80	85	90	70	75	80	70	90
Foot length	240	270	300	215	245	280	215	300
Head circumference	520	565	600	505	535	565	505	600
Head length	175	185	200	165	180	190	165	200
Head breadth	145	155	165	140	150	160	140	165

8582d

Body measurements for Region 10 (North Africa)

Measurement	Men			Women			Min.	Max.
Percentile:	5	50	95	5	50	95		
Stature	1 580	1 690	1 810	1 500	1 610	1 720	1 500	1 810
Sitting height	830	870	920	790	840	890	790	920
Eye height, sitting	700	760	820	680	740	810	680	820
Forward reach (fingertips)	800	860	920	750	810	870	750	920
Shoulder breadth (bideltoid)	390	420	460	370	410	430	370	460
Shoulder breadth (biacromial)	345	370	405	330	360	390	330	405
Hip breadth (standing)	305	330	360	320	340	380	305	380
Knee height	480	535	590	455	505	560	455	590
Lower leg length (popliteal height)	380	420	460	365	410	450	365	460
Elbow-grip length	350	375	400	330	355	380	330	400
Buttock-knee length	540	600	660	510	570	630	510	660
Buttock-heel length	950	1 030	1 120	880	960	1 050	880	1 120
Hip breadth (sitting)	310	340	370	320	350	410	310	410
Hand length	175	190	205	150	175	195	150	205
Hand breadth	90	100	110	80	95	105	80	110
Foot length	235	265	290	200	230	260	200	290
Head circumference	535	560	590	520	525	530	520	590
Head length	180	190	200	170	185	195	170	200
Head breadth	135	145	155	130	140	145	130	155

Body measurements for Region 11 (West Africa)

Measurement	Men			Women				
Percentile:	5	50	95	5	50	95	Min.	Max.
Stature	1 560	1 670	1 790	1 440	1 530	1 620	1 440	1 790
Sitting height	760	820	880	740	790	840	740	880
Eye height, sitting	650	720	780	620	680	750	620	780
Forward reach (fingertips)	790	850	900	720	760	820	720	900
Shoulder breadth (bideltoid)	390	420	450	350	390	420	350	450
Shoulder breadth (biacromial)	340	370	400	300	330	360	300	400
Hip breadth (standing)	280	310	340	300	320	350	280	350
Knee height	490	530	570	445	480	515	445	570
Lower leg length (popliteal height)	370	410	450	340	380	420	340	450
Elbow-grip length	340	370	400	300	335	350	300	400
Buttock-knee length	540	590	640	485	530	575	485	640
Buttock-heel length	940	1 020	1 090	880	960	1 045	880	1 090
Hip breadth (sitting)	290	320	350	310	340	390	290	390
Hand length	175	190	205	160	170	180	160	205
Hand breadth	80	85	90	70	75	80	70	90
Foot length	245	260	280	215	225	240	215	280
Head circumference	530	560	590	480	510	540	480	590
Head length	185	195	205	170	180	190	170	205
Head breadth	135	145	155	130	135	145	130	155

8582d

Body measurements for Region 12 (South-eastern Africa)

Measurement	Men			Women				
Percentile:	5	50	95	5	50	95	Min.	Max.
Stature	1 590	1 680	1 780	1 480	1 570	1 660	1 480	1 780
Sitting height	810	860	910	770	820	870	770	910
Eye height, sitting	700	750	790	680	730	780	680	790
Forward reach (fingertips)	810	880	950	740	800	860	740	950
Shoulder breadth (bideltoid)	390	430	460	360	395	425	360	460
Shoulder breadth (biacromial)	345	370	405	310	340	370	310	405
Hip breadth (standing)	285	315	345	300	320	360	285	360
Knee height	495	540	580	460	495	535	460	580
Lower leg length (popliteal height)	380	415	460	350	385	420	350	460
Elbow-grip length	350	380	410	300	325	350	300	410
Buttock-knee length	550	590	640	500	550	590	500	640
Buttock-heel length	940	1 020	1 100	890	970	1 050	890	1 100
Hip breadth (sitting)	290	320	350	300	340	370	290	370
Hand length	175	190	205	165	170	185	165	205
Hand breadth	80	85	90	70	75	80	70	90
Foot length	240	260	280	215	230	255	215	280
Head circumference	540	560	590	505	530	565	505	590
Head length	185	195	205	170	180	190	170	205
Head breadth	135	145	150	125	135	140	125	150

Body measurements for Region 13 (Near East)

Measurement	Men			Women			Min.	Max.
Percentile:	5	50	95	5	50	95		
Stature	1 620	1 710	1 800	1 540	1 610	1 700	1 540	1 800
Sitting height	830	890	940	800	850	900	800	940
Eye height, sitting	730	780	820	710	750	790	710	820
Forward reach (fingertips)	780	820	860	740	770	815	740	860
Shoulder breadth (bideltoid)	390	430	470	360	390	420	360	470
Shoulder breadth (biacromial)	360	380	410	330	345	370	330	410
Hip breadth (standing)	300	325	350	310	340	390	300	390
Knee height	485	520	565	460	490	510	460	565
Lower leg length (popliteal height)	400	430	460	370	400	430	370	460
Elbow-grip length	315	345	375	300	330	360	300	375
Buttock-knee length	550	580	630	520	560	600	520	630
Buttock-heel length	950	1 020	1 100	910	980	1 060	910	1 100
Hip breadth (sitting)	310	340	370	315	350	430	310	430
Hand length	175	190	205	158	170	185	158	205
Hand breadth	80	85	95	70	75	80	70	95
Foot length	245	260	285	225	240	260	225	285
Head circumference	530	550	575	500	520	550	500	575
Head length	180	190	200	170	180	190	170	200
Head breadth	140	150	160	130	140	150	130	160

8582d

Body measurements for Region 14 (North India)

Measurement	Men			Women				
Percentile:	5	50	95	5	50	95	Min.	Max.
Stature	1 580	1 670	1 770	1 450	1 540	1 630	1 450	1 770
Sitting height	820	870	920	770	820	870	770	920
Eye height, sitting	710	750	800	650	690	730	650	800
Forward reach (fingertips)	760	800	850	700	740	780	700	850
Shoulder breadth (bideltoid)	360	380	430	320	340	370	320	430
Shoulder breadth (biacromial)	350	370	390	285	310	340	285	390
Hip breadth (standing)	280	295	320	285	310	340	280	340
Knee height	500	530	560	460	490	515	460	560
Lower leg length (popliteal height)	390	415	440	360	380	410	360	440
Elbow-grip length	310	340	370	280	310	340	280	370
Buttock-knee length	550	580	620	500	530	570	500	620
Buttock-heel length	940	1 000	1 060	880	940	1 000	880	1 060
Hip breadth (sitting)	280	300	340	290	315	360	280	360
Hand length	180	190	200	150	160	170	150	200
Hand breadth	80	85	90	70	75	80	70	90
Foot length	230	250	270	205	220	235	205	270
Head circumference	515	550	580	495	525	555	495	580
Head length	180	190	200	170	180	190	170	200
Head breadth	135	145	155	125	135	145	125	155

Body measurements for Region 15 (South India)

Measurement	Men			Women			Min.	Max.
Percentile:	5	50	95	5	50	95		
Stature	1 530	1 620	1 720	1 390	1 500	1 600	1 390	1 720
Sitting height	770	820	880	740	800	850	740	880
Eye height, sitting	660	700	740	620	670	720	620	740
Forward reach (fingertips)	730	780	840	670	720	770	670	840
Shoulder breadth (bideltoid)	370	400	440	330	360	390	330	440
Shoulder breadth (biacromial)	355	375	395	310	330	350	310	395
Hip breadth (standing)	270	285	300	280	300	320	270	320
Knee height	470	510	550	440	470	505	440	550
Lower leg length (popliteal height)	380	405	430	345	375	400	345	430
Elbow-grip length	300	325	350	275	300	325	275	350
Buttock-knee length	530	560	600	480	515	550	480	600
Buttock-heel length	920	980	1 030	850	920	980	850	1 030
Hip breadth (sitting)	275	290	320	280	310	350	275	350
Hand length	180	190	200	145	155	165	145	200
Hand breadth	75	85	90	65	70	75	65	90
Foot length	225	245	265	200	215	230	200	265
Head circumference	530	550	580	475	510	540	475	580
Head length	170	180	195	165	175	185	165	195
Head breadth	135	145	150	120	130	140	120	150

8582d

Body measurements for Region 16 (North Asia)

Measurement	Men			Women			Min.	Max.
Percentile:	5	50	95	5	50	95		
Stature	1 560	1 690	1 820	1 500	1 590	1 670	1 500	1 820
Sitting height	840	900	960	800	850	900	800	960
Eye height, sitting	740	790	850	700	740	790	700	850
Forward reach (fingertips)	780	840	900	720	790	850	720	900
Shoulder breadth (bideltoid)	390	430	460	360	390	430	360	460
Shoulder breadth (biacromial)	355	390	420	320	350	380	320	420
Hip breadth (standing)	300	325	355	305	335	375	300	375
Knee height	475	515	555	440	475	515	440	555
Lower leg length (popliteal height)	375	405	440	350	385	415	350	440
Elbow-grip length	305	340	380	295	315	350	295	380
Buttock-knee length	500	550	600	480	530	580	480	600
Buttock-heel length	920	1 020	1 110	900	980	1 060	900	1 110
Hip breadth (sitting)	310	340	370	310	350	380	310	380
Hand length	180	195	210	165	180	195	165	210
Hand breadth	85	90	100	75	85	90	75	100
Foot length	230	250	280	205	225	240	205	280
Head circumference	515	550	590	510	540	570	510	590
Head length	175	190	205	170	180	185	170	205
Head breadth	140	150	165	135	145	150	135	165

Body measurements for Region 17 (South China)

Measurement	Men			Women				
Percentile:	5	50	95	5	50	95	Min.	Max.
Stature	1 610	1 660	1 710	1 430	1 520	1 590	1 430	1 710
Sitting height	790	840	890	740	790	840	740	890
Eye height, sitting	690	740	790	650	690	740	650	790
Forward reach (fingertips)	760	800	840	690	730	760	690	840
Shoulder breadth (bideltoid)	365	400	425	335	360	395	335	425
Shoulder breadth (biacromial)	340	360	395	310	330	355	310	395
Hip breadth (standing)	285	310	330	305	330	360	285	360
Knee height	490	505	520	415	460	490	415	520
Lower leg length (popliteal height)	370	400	430	330	370	400	330	430
Elbow-grip length	315	335	360	280	305	335	280	360
Buttock-knee length	500	540	580	460	490	520	460	580
Buttock-heel length	970	1 010	1 040	880	940	1 000	880	1 040
Hip breadth (sitting)	295	320	340	330	370	410	295	410
Hand length	165	180	195	150	165	180	150	195
Hand breadth	90	95	100	80	85	90	80	100
Foot length	230	245	260	210	225	240	210	260
Head circumference	530	550	570	510	535	555	510	570
Head length	180	190	200	170	180	190	170	200
Head breadth	140	150	160	135	145	150	135	160

8582d

Body measurements for Region 18 (South-East Asia)

Measurement	Men			Women				
Percentile:	5	50	95	5	50	95	Min.	Max.
Stature	1 530	1 630	1 720	1 440	1 530	1 620	1 440	1 720
Sitting height	790	840	900	750	800	850	750	900
Eye height, sitting	680	730	780	660	700	740	660	780
Forward reach (fingertips)	730	780	820	690	730	780	690	820
Shoulder breadth (bideltoid)	380	410	430	340	380	410	340	430
Shoulder breadth (biacromial)	320	370	420	300	335	370	300	420
Hip breadth (standing)	285	310	330	285	315	360	285	360
Knee height	465	495	525	430	460	485	430	525
Lower leg length (popliteal height)	380	415	445	365	385	405	365	445
Elbow-grip length	300	325	360	280	305	340	280	360
Buttock-knee length	490	530	570	470	500	530	470	570
Buttock-heel length	910	970	1 025	860	915	970	860	1 025
Hip breadth (sitting)	290	315	340	330	365	400	290	400
Hand length	160	175	185	155	165	175	155	185
Hand breadth	75	80	85	70	75	80	70	85
Foot length	220	235	250	210	220	235	210	250
Head circumference	530	565	595	500	530	560	500	595
Head length	175	185	195	165	175	185	165	195
Head breadth	135	145	155	130	135	145	130	155

Body measurements for Region 19 (Australia – European population)

Measurement	Men			Women				
Percentile:	5	50	95	5	50	95	Min.	Max.
Stature	1 660	1 770	1 890	1 560	1 670	1 770	1 560	1 890
Sitting height	880	930	980	830	880	930	830	980
Eye height, sitting	760	810	860	710	760	810	710	860
Forward reach (fingertips)	800	860	920	740	800	860	740	920
Shoulder breadth (bideltoid)	410	450	490	350	380	420	350	490
Shoulder breadth (biacromial)	350	390	420	320	345	370	320	420
Hip breadth (standing)	300	330	360	310	350	400	300	400
Knee height	530	570	600	480	525	565	480	600
Lower leg length (popliteal height)	405	440	475	365	400	440	365	475
Elbow-grip length	325	360	400	300	335	370	300	400
Buttock-knee length	570	610	660	540	580	630	540	660
Buttock-heel length	1 000	1 090	1 180	950	1 030	1 100	950	1 180
Hip breadth (sitting)	310	340	370	320	360	430	310	430
Hand length	175	190	205	160	175	190	160	205
Hand breadth	80	90	95	70	75	85	70	95
Foot length	250	265	280	220	240	260	220	280
Head circumference	530	565	600	515	545	570	515	600
Head length	180	192	200	170	180	190	170	200
Head breadth	145	155	165	135	145	155	135	165

Body measurements for Region 20 (Japan)

Measurement	Men			Women			Min.	Max.
Percentile:	5	50	95	5	50	95		
Stature	1 630	1 720	1 820	1 510	1 590	1 670	1 510	1 820
Sitting height	850	920	1 000	790	860	930	790	1 000
Eye height, sitting	750	820	880	690	750	820	690	880
Forward reach (fingertips)	800	850	900	750	790	830	750	900
Shoulder breadth (bideltoid)	380	420	450	330	370	410	330	450
Shoulder breadth (biacromial)	340	370	400	300	340	380	300	400
Hip breadth (standing)	305	320	340	310	330	360	305	360
Knee height	470	515	560	445	470	495	445	560
Lower leg length (popliteal height)	390	415	440	375	395	415	375	440
Elbow-grip length	320	345	380	295	320	350	295	380
Buttock-knee length	530	560	600	500	530	580	500	600
Buttock-heel length	950	1 030	1 110	920	970	1 020	920	1 110
Hip breadth (sitting)	305	325	350	310	330	360	305	360
Hand length	170	185	200	140	170	180	140	200
Hand breadth	80	85	95	70	80	85	70	95
Foot length	230	245	260	210	225	240	210	260
Head circumference	520	555	570	515	545	560	515	570
Head length	175	190	200	170	180	190	170	200
Head breadth	145	155	160	140	145	155	140	160

Region 1: North America

Canada
United States

Population of the region: 261 million

Data sources:

Abraham, S. et al. (1976, 1979)
Alexander, M. and Clauser, C.E. (1965)
Bailey, D.A. et al. (1982)
Borkan, G.A. and Norris, A.H. (1977)
Borkan, G.A. et al. (1983)
Clarke, M.F. (1971)
Clauser, C. et al. (1972)
Damon, A. (1966)
Damon, A. and Thomas, R.B. (1967)
Department of Defense (ed.) (1980)
Friedlaender, J.S. et al. (1977)
Garrett, J.W. (1970)
Grunhofer, H.J. and Kroh, G. (eds.) (1975)
Hamill, P.V.V. et al. (1973)
Hertzberg, H.T.E. et al. (1954)
Karpinos, B.D. (1961)
Knapik, J.J. (1983)
Koh, E.T. (1981)
Little, J.A. et al. (1986)
Malina, R.M. et al. (1983)
Novak, L.P. (1970)
Pollitzer, W.S. et al. (1970)
Pollock, M.L. (1975)
Pomerance, H.H. and Krall, J.M. (1985)
Robbins, D.H. and Reynolds, H.M. (1975)
Salvendy, G. (1971)
Scott, E.C. and Bajema, C.J. (1982)
Snyder, R.G. et al. (1977)
Song, T.M. and Garvie, G.T. (1980)
Stoudt, H.W. and Damon, A. (1960)
Stoudt, H.W. et al. (1965)
Weisz, J.D. (1968)
White, R. (1982)

Region 2:   Latin America (Indian population)

        Bolivia
        Colombia
        Ecuador
        El Salvador
        Guatemala
        Honduras
        Mexico
        Nicaragua
        Panama
        Paraguay
        Peru
        Venezuela

        Population of the region: 201 million

Data sources:

Diaz Ungria, A.G. et al. (1956)
Frisancho, R.A. et al. (1975)
Gusinde, M. (1956)
Hass, J. et al. (1980)
Lasker, G.W. (1962)
Lasker, G.W. and Thomas, R. (1976)
Leatherman, T.L. et al. (1984)
Lehmann, H. and Marquer, P. (1960)
Little, B.B. and Malina, R.M. (1986)
Maksud, M.G. et al. (1976)
Martorell, R. et al. (1981)
Mendez, J. and Behrhorst, C. (1963)
Mueller, W.H. et al. (1980)
Ruffie, T. et al. (1966)
Russell, M. (1976)
Salzano, F.M. (ed.) (1971)
Sandoval Arriaga, A. (1980)
Stefano, G.F. de and Jenkins, J.M. (1973)
Vargas, G.L.A. et al. (1976)
Vellard, J. (1951)

Region 3: Latin America (European-Negroid population)

Argentina
Belize
Brazil
Chile
Costa Rica
French Guyana
Guyana
Suriname
Uruguay
Caribbean Island States

Population of the region: 181 million

Data sources:

Davies, B.T. et al. (1980)
Eveleth, P.B. (1972)
Glanville, E.V. and Geerdink, R.A. (1970)
Halberstein, R.A. and Davies, J.E. (1984)
Hiba, J.C. and Luco, M.F. de (1982)
Kuyp, E. van der (1967)
Laska-Mierzejewska, T. (1967, 1970)
Neves, W.A. (1985)
Palomino, H. et al. (1979)
Pollitzer, W.S. et al. (1982)
Rocha, F.J. da and Salzano, F.M. (1972)
Rothhammer, F. and Spielmann, R.S. (1972)
Valenzuela, C.Y. and Avendano, A.B. (1979)
Valenzuela, C.Y. and Rothhammer, F. (1978)

Region 4:   Northern Europe

    Denmark
    Finland
    Federal Republic of Germany
    Iceland
    Ireland
    Netherlands
    Norway
    Sweden

    Population of the region: 102 million

Data sources:

Atterhög, J.-H. et al. (1980)
Berglund, L. et al. (1974)
Bjelke, E. (1971)
Brekelmans, F.E.M. et al. (1986)
Danmarks Statistik (1984)
Deutsches Institut für Normung (1979)
Finger, G. and Harbeck, R. (1961)
Grunhofer, H.J. and Kroh, G. (eds.) (1975)
Ingelmark, E. and Lewin, T. (1966, 1968)
Institut für Wehrmedizinalstatistik und Berichtswesen (Hg.) (1975)
Kurth, G. and Lam, T.H. (1969)
Kvasnicka, E.W. and Radl, G.W. (1977)
Lewin, T. (1969)
Lewin, T. and Skrobak-Kaczynski, J. (1972)
Molenbroek, J.M. et al. (1983)
Mustakallio, M. and Telkkä, A. (1951)
Noppa, H. et al. (1979, 1980)
Nordgren, B. (1972)
Nylind, B. et al. (1978)
Norges offisielle statistikk (1984a, b)
Prokopec, M. (1969)
Schmidtke, H. and Jürgens, H.W. (Hg.) (1975)
Telkkä, A. (1952)
Udjus, L.G. (1964)
Watson, A.W.S. (1981)

Region 5: Central Europe

   Austria
   Belgium
   Czechoslovakia
   German Democratic Republic
   Luxembourg
   Switzerland (including Liechtenstein)
   United Kingdom

   Population of the region: 106 million

Data sources:

Anderson, W.F. and Cowan, N.R. (1965)
Beckers, R. and Pleysier, R. (1980)
Board of Trade (ed.) (1957)
British Standards Institution (1969)
Carver, N. et al. (1986)
Chmelar, J. (1967)
Clements, E.M.B. and Pickett, K.G. (1957)
Cvicelova, M. (1983)
Davies, B.T. et al. (1980a, 1980b)
Delwaide, P.A. et al. (1973)
Durnin, J.V.G.A. and Womersley, J. (1974)
Flügel, B. et al. (1986)
Grandjean, E. and Burandt, U. (1962)
Harrison, J.M. and Marshall, W.A. (1970)
Haslegrave, C.M. (1979, 1980)
Heimendinger, J. (1964)
Heyters, C. (1983)
Ince, N.E. et al. (1973)
Miall, W.E. et al. (1967)
Morant, G.M. (1956)
Morant, G.M. and Ruffell Smith, H.P. (1947)
Morant, G.M. et al. (1952)
Parizkova, J. and Eiselt, E. (1971, 1980)
Pheasant, S. (1986)
Richardson, J.F. and Pincherle, G. (1969)
Roberts, D.F. (1960)
Rosenbaum, S. et al. (1985)
R.A.F. Institute of Aviation Medicine (1956)
Seidler, H. (1986)
Simpson, R.E. and Bolton, C.B. (1968)
Sporcq, J. (1969)
Strelka, F. et al. (1979)
Susanne, C. (1980)
Susanne, C. and Heyne, D. (1972)
Ward, J.S. (1965)
Ward, J.S. and Kirk, N.S. (1967, 1970)
Wright, H.B. (1968)
Zentralstelle für Standardisierung (1976)

Region 6: Eastern Europe

Poland
Soviet Union (European part)

Population of the region: 226 million

Data sources:

Antropometriceskij Atlas (1977)
Barancewicz, J. and Niemiec, S. (1974a, 1974b)
Batogowska, A. and Slowikowski, J. (1974)
Bielicki, T. et al. (1981)
Gorny, S. (1972)
Heeneberg, M. (1985)
Kopczynski, J. (1972a, 1972b)
Metodiceskie rekomendacii (1982)
Nowak, E. (1976)
Polska Akademia Nauk, Komisja Antropometrii (ed.) (1962)
Wolanski, N. and Pyzuk, M. (1973)
Wolanski, N. et al. (1975)

Region 7: South-eastern Europe

Bulgaria
Greece
Hungary
Israel
Italy
Malta
Romania
Yugoslavia

Population of the region: 137 million

Data sources:

Botezatu, D. et al. (1981)
Brian, L. and Guerci, A. (1979)
Brian, L. et al. (1984)
Corrain, C. (1956, 1962, 1965, 1976)
Corrain, C. et al. (1962, 1969, 1973, 1974)
Correnti, V. (1969)
Erishman, F.F. (1959)
Ente Italiano della Moda (1979)
Floris, G. et al. (1986)
Gavrilovic, Z. and Badojevic, P. (1984)
Guerci, A. (1977)
Hertzberg, H.T.E. et al. (1963)
Jürgens, H.W. and Pieper, U. (1984)
Kadanov, D. and Pandova, B. (1967)
Kadanov, D. and Mutafov, S. (1967a, 1967b, 1977)
Kadanov, D. et al. (1979)
Locati, G. et al. (1977)
Marotta, M. (1954)
Masali, M. (1977)
Maxia, C. and Fenu, A. (1963a, 1963b, 1967)
Papai, J. (1978)
Parizkova, J. and Buzkova, P. (1971)
Parizkova, J. and Eiselt, E. (1966)
Pisl, Z. et al. (1980)
Radu, E. and Lungu, C. (1981)
Reginato, E. et al. (1961)
Rudan, P. et al. (1986)
Soleo, L. et al. (1980)
Valoras, V.G. (1970)
Vascotto, G. (1972)

Region 8: France

Population of the region: 55 million

Data sources:

Bernard, M. and Hueber, A. (1968, 1969)
Bouisset, S. and Monod, H. (1961)
Bouisset, S. et al. (1960)
CETIH (1968)
CERRA (1973)
Chabeuf, M. (1964)
Chamla, M.-C. (1964)
Création de modeles tridimensionelles de pilotes (1984)
Estryn, M. et al. (1976)
Marquer, P. and Chamla, M.-C. (1961)
Martuzzi, F. (1968)
Monod, H. and Wisner, A. (1964)
Olivier, G. (1975)
Olivier, G. and Devigne, G. (1985)
Olivier, G. et al. (1957, 1977a, 1977b)
Wisner, A. and Rebiffe, R. (1963)
Wisner, A. et al. (1974)

Region 9: Iberian Peninsula

Portugal
Spain

Population of the region: 49 million

Data sources:

Dobon, L.C. (1977)
Gomez, P.G. (1976, 1978)
Palacios Mateos, J.M. et al. (1978)
Riesco, J.A. (1979)
Vidal, A.A. et al. (1982)

Region 10:   North Africa

    Algeria
    Chad
    Egypt
    Ethiopia
    Libyan Arab Jamahariya
    Mali
    Mauritania
    Morocco
    Niger
    Spanish Sahara
    Sudan
    Tunisia

    Population of the region: 177 million

Data sources:

Dellaportas, G.J. (1969)
Moustafa, A.W. et al. (1987)
Peters, W.-H. et al. (1987)
Sahbi, N. (1983, 1985)
Sprynar, Z. et al. (1970)
Strouhal, E. (1970, 1971)
Sukkar, M.Y. (1976)
Wiercinski, A. (1970)

Region 11: West Africa

Benin
Burkina Faso
Cameroon
Central African Republic
Congo
Côte d'Ivoire
Equatorial Guinea
Gabon
Gambia
Ghana
Guinea
Guinea-Bissau
Liberia
Nigeria
Sierra Leone
Togo
Zaire

Population of the region: 194 million

Data sources:

Austin, D.M. et al. (1979)
Correnti, V. et al. (1973)
Cresta, M. (1985)
Cessain, M. (1979)
Hiernaux, J. (1956, 1964, 1965)
Huizinga, J. (1968)
Lestrange, M. de (1950)
Lestrange, M.-Th. (1977)

Region 12:   South-eastern Africa

Angola
Botswana
Burundi
Kenya
Lesotho
Madagascar
Malawi
Mozambique
Namibia
Rwanda
Somalia
South Africa
Swaziland
Uganda
United Republic of Tanzania
Zambia
Zimbabwe

Population of the region: 161 million

Data sources:

Ashby, P. (1978)
Castro e Almeida, M. de (1956)
Chabeuf, M. (1969)
Cristescu, M. et al. (1978)
Davies, C.T.M. et al. (1973)
Keller, W. and Kopf, H. (1963)
Knussmann, R. and Knussmann, E. (1970)
Latham, M.C. et al. (1982)
Morrison, J.F. (1965)
Morrison, J.F. et al. (1968)
Nurse, G.T. (1971)
Santos David, J.H. (1972)
Slome, C. et al. (1960)
Tobias, P.V. (1971)
Villiers, H. de (1971)
Walker, A.R.P. and Walker, B.F. (1977)

Region 13: Near East

Afghanistan
Bahrain
Iraq
Islamic Republic of Iran
Jordan
Kuwait
Lebanon
Oman
People's Democratic Republic of Yemen
Qatar
Saudi Arabia
Syrian Arab Republic
Turkey
United Arab Emirates
Yemen Arab Republic

Population of the region: 165 million

Data sources:

Debetz, G.J. (1969)
Hertzberg, H.T.E. et al. (1963)
Ikeda, Jiro (1960)
Jürgens, H.W. and Pieper, U. (1984)
Mooij, D. (1972)

Region 14:   North India

   Bangladesh
   Bhutan
   India (northern part)
   Nepal
   Pakistan

   Population of the region: 492 million

Data sources:

Balgir, R.S. (1985)
Bharadwaj, H. et al. (1977)
Chopra, S.R.K. (1969)
Clarke, M.F. (1966a, 1966b, 1971)
Das, B.M. et al. (1985a, 1985b, 1986a, 1986b, 1986c)
Davies, B.T. et al. (1980b)
Duggal, N. and Nath, S. (1986)
Hauser, G. and Wytek, R. (1983)
Kanda, S. (1966)
Mavalwala, J. (1966)
McConnel, W. et al. (1985)
Satwanti, H. et al. (1978)
Sen, R.N. et al. (1977)
Sidhu, L.S. and Kansal, D.K. (1974)
Singal, P. and Sidhu, L.S. (1987)
Singh, S.P. (1981)
Sloan, A.W. and Masali, M. (1978)

Region 15:   South India

        India (southern part)
        Maldives
        Sri Lanka

        Population of the region: 412 million

Data sources:

Cullumbine, H. et al. (1950)
Sen, R.N. (1964)
Stoudt, H.W. (1961)

Region 16:   North Asia

China (northern part)
Mongolia
Soviet Union (Asian part)

Population of the region: 690 million

Data sources:

Anthropologisches Institut Kiel (1986)
Shao, Xinzhou et al. (1984)
Suzuki, H. and Kouchi, M. (1986)
Xu, Jiujin and Du, Roufu (1985)
Zolotareva, I.M. (1969)

Region 17: South China

> China (southern part)
> Hong Kong
> Macao
> Taiwan, China
>
> Population of the region: 425 million

Data sources:

Chen, K.P. et al. (1963)
Courtney, A.J. (1984)
Courtney, A.J. and Ng, M.K. (1984)
Kimura, K. and Tsai, C. (1967, 1968)
Nakata, S. (1987b)
Tsai, Tsuli et al. (1969)
Wang, Chien-Che (1984)
Yuan, Chung-Yin (1982)

Region 18:   South-East Asia

        Brunei
        Democratic Kampuchea
        Indonesia
        Lao People's Democratic Republic
        Malaysia
        Myanmar
        Philippines
        Singapore
        Thailand
        Viet Nam

        Population of the region: 391 million

Data sources:

Anh, Tran and Tien-Loi, Vu (1966)
Chabeuf, M. (1967)
Huard, P. et al. (1962)
Krukoff, S. (1966)
Kurth, G. and Lam, T.H. (1969)
Lee, J. et al. (1981)
Lourie, J.A. and Taufa, T. (1986)
Novak, L.P. (1970)
Olivier, G. (1956)
Ringrose, H. and Zimmet, P. (1979)
Rutishauser, I.H.E. and McCay, H. (1986)

Region 19: Australia (European population)

Australia
New Zealand

Population of the region: 19 million

Data sources:

Bullock, M.I. and Steinberg, M. (1975)
Hanna, J.M. and Baker, P.T. (1979)
Hughes, J.G. and Lomaev, O. (1972)
Lee, J. et al. (1981)
McGarvey, S.T. and Baker, P.T. (1979)
Watson, P.E. et al. (1980)

Region 20: Japan

Democratic Republic of Korea
Japan
Republic of Korea

Population of the region: 160 million

Data sources:

Ashizawa, K. et al. (1986)
Imabayashi, M. and Kanda, S. (1982, 1983, 1984a, 1984b)
Imabayashi, M. and Watanabe, T. (1984)
Imabayashi, M. et al. (1982, 1984)
Kimura, K. (1984)
Lee, S.D. (1978)
Miyashita, T. and Takahashi, E. (1971)
Morimote, T. (1986)
Morimoto, T. et al. (1982)
Morimoto, Y. and Kanda, S. (1983)
Morita, S. and Ohtsuki, F. (1973)
Nagamine, S. and Suzuki, S. (1964)
Nakata, S. (1987a)
Nakata, S. and Kanda, S. (1987)
Nakata, S. et al. (1985, 1986, 1987)
Ohyama, S. et al. (1987)
Picon-Reategui, E. et al. (1979)
Song, T.M. and Garvie, G.T. (1980)
Takai, S. and Shimaguchi, S. (1986)
Yanagisawa, S. (1961)

7. The possibilities of type classification

It was already clear in Chapter 3 that there were numerous possible ways to adapt working environments and consumer goods to the great variations in human body measurements – and, indeed, numerous attempts have been made. At the same time, it was also noted that an extension of this adaptation to cover large parts of the world's population would run up against substantial difficulties. Generally speaking, it is not sensible either ergonomically, technically or from the economic standpoint to try, as has so far been the case, to achieve a world-wide metrical adaptation solely on the basis of adjustability. It is much more desirable to attempt a classification of at least two basic types, and thereafter to move towards adaptation by providing for adjustments.

The following are the requirements for an adaptation of this kind:

- all numerically important populations which are involved in international exchanges should be taken into account;

- the breakdown must take equal account of both sexes;

- the breakdown must cover all relevant body measurements of the populations included, from the fifth to the 95th percentiles.

As the problem of adaptation by adjustment mechanisms has in theory been solved and enough experience in this field is available, we concentrate here on a possible subdivision into types – two in the first instance. In so doing, we set the condition that this type classification should meet the above-listed requirements as far as possible equally for all regions.

7.1 Populations and body measurements to be taken into account

The anthropometric studies available on the world population have been grouped together in the world compilation on the basis of 20 regional groups. To arrive at a meaningful type classification, this number must be reduced even further. In so doing, it is desirable to apply to any further merging of groups the same principles as governed the classification into these 20 regional groups. Here the regional location is less important, the vital factors being the anthropometric ones, including body proportions. On this basis, it is for example possible to group together European populations from different parts of the world.

In this way, we arrive at the following nine groups:

- the Northern European Group (NEU): the populations of North America, Northern Europe, Central Europe, Eastern Europe and Australia (European population);

- the Southern European Group (SEU): the populations of France, the Iberian Peninsula, South-eastern Europe and Latin America (European-Negroid population);

- the Near East Group (NAO): the populations of the Near East and North Africa;

- the African Group (AFR): the populations of Western and South-eastern Africa;

- the South-East Asian Group (SOA): the populations of South China and South-East Asia;

- the Japanese Group (JAP): the population of Japan;

- the North Asian Group (NAS): the populations of North Asia;

- the Indian Group (IND): the populations of North and South India; and

- the South American Group (SAM): the Indians of Latin America.

As it is clear from the body measurements contained in the world compilation that the variation within groups exceeds the variation between groups we have subdivided each of the nine groups by sex. We shall therefore consider nine male and nine female partial populations within the above-mentioned groups.

As all the measurements given in the world compilation are ergonomically important, one possibility of type classification would lie in checking each individual measurement. However, since there are correlations between different body measurements, we can arrive at a classification from the ergonomic standpoint by using a reduced combination of features limited to the so-called indicative measurements. Stature, which is frequently used as the sole indicative measurement, is unsuitable for the present purposes. The world compilation shows that the body proportions of the different races clearly vary (e.g. a higher trunk proportion among Mongolians and a higher leg proportion among Negroids), so that an attempt to use stature as the only indicator would inevitably lead to wrong groupings. Stature is only seldom used directly in determining the dimensions of workplaces and consumer goods; its practical importance is considerably less than that of other body measurements.

For investigating the possibilities of type classification, it seems appropriate therefore to use a manageable combination of as few body measurements as possible, taking those which are particularly relevant in practice and are also suitable as indicator measurements. When considering what is of practical relevance, it is desirable to base oneself on workstations involving a sitting position and in this context to take as the most important elements the height of the trunk over the seating surface (sitting height, trunk length), the length of the segment of the body which is on the seat (buttock-knee length) and the length of the body segment from the base level to the seating surface (lower leg length (popliteal height)). In addition, those measurements which most characterise bodily shape, namely shoulder breadth and hip breadth (sitting) should be considered. As the most frequent measurement recorded world-wide is stature, it is desirable also to take this into account as an additional indicator when distinguishing the different types.

7.2 Subdivision of the populations into ergonomic-anthropometric groups

The subdivision into groups necessary for the planned classification should be carried out by using a bundle of characteristics rather than isolated measurements. Figures 1 and 2 show the mean values for men and women in each of these nine groups for sitting height and buttock-knee length. The line linking the mean values of a population corresponds to the extent of sex differentiation. We have calculated the value for the vertical line of separation TL by means of the formula

$$TL = \bar{x}_{min} + ((\bar{x}_{max} - \bar{x}_{min})/2).$$

Figure 1 leads to the following two-group classification. The group with the higher measurements includes the Northern and Southern Europeans, the North Asians and the Japanese group. The group with the lower measurements covers the Africans, people from India and from South-East Asia and the South American Indians. The population of the Near East (including North Africa) occupies an intermediate position. If we now compare the data from figure 2 with these results, we find another grouping. The Northern and Southern Europeans and the populations of South-East Asia and South America can be ranked together without difficulty in relation to the separation line. But here, the Africans and the Near Eastern populations fall into the group characterised by higher measurements, while the North Asians come into the group with smaller measurements. The Indians and the Japanese group occupy an intermediate position in relation to this measurement. The comparison of figures 1 and 2 makes it clear that group differentiation on the basis of isolated body measurements leads nowhere. We must instead go for a combination of features.

Figure 1. <u>Differences in mean value of sitting height between men
and women in nine population groups (measured in mm)</u>
(The left- and right-hand ends of each horizontal line
represent in each case the measurements for women and
for men respectively.)

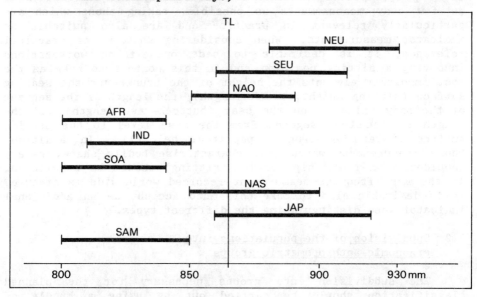

Figure 2. <u>Differences in mean value of buttock-knee length
between men and women in nine population groups
(measured in mm).</u>
(The left- and right-hand ends of each horizontal line
represent in each case the measurements for women and
for men respectively.)

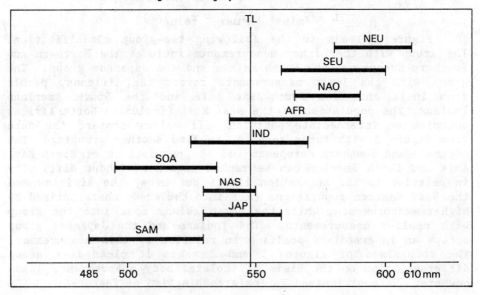

In separating the groups, one must consider that the variation of body measurements within groups is greater than the variation between the groups. In relation to this, the scatter of body measurements must be taken into account in separating the groups. It therefore seems plausible, taking account of all six indicator measurements mentioned above, to separate the measurement pattern at a defined point between P5 and P95 which, in each case, are to be understood as the minimum and maximum measurements. Unfortunately, objective criteria for such a procedure are lacking and, therefore, distribution into groups would be more or less arbitrary. It is also significant that for the indicator measurements we know the arithmetical mean and the standard deviation, as well as the fifth and 95th percentiles, but we do not have individual values for each measurement and for each population. This excludes the use of advanced statistical procedures for group formation and group separation such as cluster analysis or discrimination analysis with calculation of the generalised distance according to Mahalanobis. It is therefore appropriate to select a procedure which includes measurements of distances between groups, but does not require the existence of individual values: instead, only the mean values and scatter measurements (i.e. the so-called Penrose distance) are necessary. The distance measurements thus calculated provide a sufficiently accurate picture of the available data. There is a 0.97 correlation between the results of group separation which were obtained by Mahalanobis and by Penrose's procedure (Knussmann, 1967).

Calculation of the Penrose distances on the basis of the six indicator measurements leads to the distance matrix shown in table 1 for the nine populations groups considered.

Table 1. Matrix of Penrose distances between nine
          population groups (on the basis of six body
          measurements)

	NEU	SEU	NAO	AFR	IND	SOA	NAS	JAP	SAM
NEU	–								
SEU	0.09	–							
NAO	0.20	0.11	–						
AFR	0.69	0.38	0.17	–					
IND	0.83	0.57	0.33	0.28	–				
SOA	1.39	0.98	0.80	0.77	0.95	–			
NAS	0.59	0.35	0.49	0.73	0.70	0.32	–		
JAP	0.47	0.43	0.42	0.72	0.41	0.89	0.43	–	
SAM	1.52	0.93	0.90	0.70	0.74	0.83	0.74	1.01	–

In order to have an overall picture of all the distances a dendrogram was calculated on the basis of this matrix to show all the numerical data diagramatically (figure 3).

Figure 3. Dendrogram of Penrose distances between nine population groups (on the basis of six body measurements)

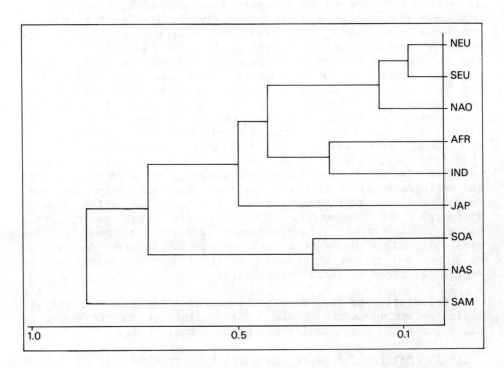

In figure 3 one can immediately recognise three paired groups: North and South Europeans, Africans and Indians, South-East Asians and North Asians. The populations from the Near East are close to the European block. There is also a relationship between this large block and the African-Indian group. To this relationship can be added populations from Japan, together with the South-East Asia-North Asia block. The South American Indians are comparatively some distance away.

This calculation does not take sexual differences into account, as the distance calculations have so far been reckoned for men and women together in each population. A glance at the world compilation shows, however, that the differences between the sexes are considerable. We have therefore calculated a second dendrogram (figure 4) showing the female and male groups as separate populations in the distance calculation. The distance matrix used as the basis for this dendrogram is given in table 2.

68   8593d

Table 2. Matrix of Penrose distances between nine population groups subdivided by sex (on the basis of six body measurements)

	NEU♂	NEU♀	SEU♂	SEU♀	NAO♂	NAO♀	AFR♂	AFR♀	IND♂	IND♀	SOA♂	SOA♀	NAS♂	NAS♀	JAP♂	JAP♀	SAM♂	SAM♀
NEU♂	–																	
NEU♀	1.15	–																
SEU♂	0.05	0.78	–															
SEU♀	1.66	0.20	1.16	–														
NAO♂	0.31	0.64	0.14	0.95	–													
NAO♀	1.42	0.18	0.90	0.21	0.51	–												
AFR♂	0.75	1.05	0.49	1.18	0.19	0.66	–											
AFR♀	2.48	0.78	1.66	0.42	1.22	0.25	1.13	–										
IND♂	0.93	1.14	0.70	1.41	0.43	0.76	0.26	1.61	–									
IND♀	2.74	0.82	2.06	0.56	1.35	0.46	1.48	0.33	1.58	–								
SOA♂	1.19	0.91	0.80	1.01	0.45	0.59	0.61	1.05	0.55	1.02	–							
SOA♀	5.29	1.79	4.22	1.45	3.82	1.49	4.44	1.06	5.43	1.46	3.28	–						
NAS♂	0.78	0.52	0.53	0.60	0.52	0.61	1.02	1.13	1.05	1.07	0.42	2.53	–					
NAS♀	2.75	0.46	2.15	0.32	1.83	0.52	2.37	0.58	2.59	0.49	1.61	0.47	0.96	–				
JAP♂	0.58	1.11	0.51	1.45	0.53	1.19	0.90	2.12	0.65	1.84	0.51	4.76	0.34	2.22	–			
JAP♀	1.60	0.44	1.18	0.60	0.82	0.36	1.23	0.68	1.19	0.42	0.56	1.70	0.35	0.54	0.88	–		
SAM♂	1.45	1.79	1.11	1.58	1.10	1.51	1.10	1.83	1.14	2.18	0.82	4.47	0.82	2.70	1.07	1.51	–	
SAM♀	3.38	1.68	2.83	1.02	2.11	0.95	2.16	0.44	2.49	0.48	1.46	1.02	1.47	0.71	2.79	1.03	1.88	–

♂ = male; ♀ = female.

Figure 4 clearly shows a separation into two groups, one for men and one for women. This immediately indicates that the sex differences in all ethnic and regional groups are greater than the differences related to racial origin. Within the male block, there are three subgroups: a European group, a group consisting of Indians, Africans and the population of the Near East, and another group which is Mongolian in the broadest sense. Here, too, the Indians of South America are relatively isolated.

Figure 4. <u>Dendrogram of Penrose distances between nine population groups subdivided by sex (on the basis of six body measurements)</u>

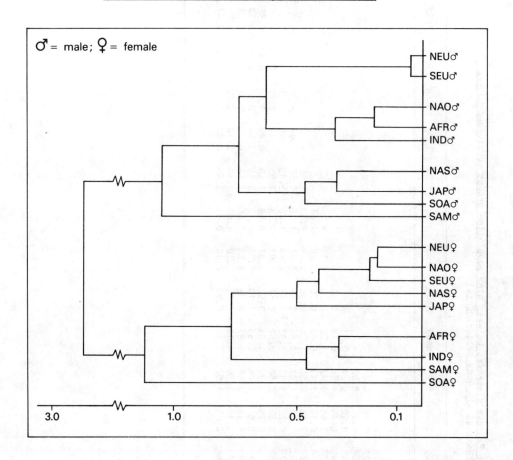

Within the female block the picture is more heterogeneous, although two major subgroups can be broadly distinguished. The first consists of Europeans and populations from the Near East, together with populations from North Asia and Japan. In the second subgroup come Africans, Indians, South American Indians and populations from South-East Asia. Overall, it emerges that separate consideration of the two sexes leads to a different constitution of groups from that produced by calculation of distances based on a combined value for a population covering both sexes together.

This very clear biometric result is of little help in classifying workstations by size world-wide, as a subdivision of workstations for men and women respectively cannot be the purpose of a metrical breakdown of the world population.

In evaluating these results, one must bear in mind that the combination of characteristics used here consists of four length and two breadth measurements. It is, however, well known that the length measurements have relatively high correlations with one another, as do the breadth measurements, but that the correlations between length and breadth measurements are much looser. In this connection, it is important to note that breadth measurements are much more affected by sex differentiation. The relationship between shoulder breadth and pelvis, hip or seat breadth is a particularly significant sex indicator. From the ergonomic standpoint, when the relative importance of length and breadth measurements is considered, the length measurements clearly take priority. Range of vision, reach, and foot space are all determined by length measurements. Breadth measurements, on the other hand, are less important for the design workstations. In view of the unmethodological basis on which the results are founded, it is desirable to rely only on the four length measurements for subdivision into groups.

The corresponding distance measurements are given in table 3 and the dendrogram in figure 5. These produce the following group structures: the "male block" referred to in figure 4, includes two female populations, women from Northern Europe and women from the Near East. The male group of South American Indians, which already appeared atypical in figures 3 and 4, is now part of the female block. There are therefore three blocks: the first comprises Northern and Southern European men, men from India, the Near East and Africa, together with women from Northern Europe and the Near East. The second block consists of the male populations from the Far East: North Asia, Japan and South-East Asia. The third block is composed of the male South American Indians and the remaining female populations. If one confines oneself to a separation into two groups, then it is reasonable to combine the first and second blocks into a single one, as can be seen from the dendrogram. One assumes, however, that the male populations from the Far East occupy an intermediate position between the two blocks in terms of measurements. In order to illustrate this, figure 6 shows the ranges of the smallest P5 up to the largest P95 for all four length measurements for the three blocks from figure 5.

Table 3. Matrix of Penrose distances between nine population groups subdivided by sex (on the basis of four length measurements)

	NEU♂	NEU♀	SEU♂	SEU♀	NAO♂	NAO♀	AFR♂	AFR♀	IND♂	IND♀	SOA♂	SOA♀	NAS♂	NAS♀	JAP♂	JAP♀	SAM♂	SAM♀
NEU♂	–																	
NEU♀	0.37	–																
SEU♂	0.03	0.17	–															
SEU♀	0.78	0.13	0.51	–														
NAO♂	0.29	0.09	0.12	0.36	–													
NAO♀	0.86	0.16	0.48	0.21	0.20	–												
AFR♂	0.80	0.35	0.49	0.50	0.18	0.21	–											
AFR♀	1.82	0.65	1.18	0.48	0.71	0.19	0.45	–										
IND♂	0.66	0.14	0.36	0.33	0.10	0.04	0.12	0.29	–									
IND♀	1.96	0.67	1.38	0.39	0.98	0.34	0.88	0.13	0.69	–								
SOA♂	1.04	0.47	0.68	0.61	0.59	0.40	0.72	0.58	0.45	0.72	–							
SOA♀	2.74	1.39	2.09	1.36	1.55	0.93	1.82	0.64	1.60	0.60	0.72	–						
NAS♂	0.63	0.33	0.49	0.42	0.73	0.66	1.14	1.11	0.72	0.89	0.40	1.10	–					
NAS♀	1.24	0.38	0.89	0.25	0.60	0.37	0.98	0.46	0.66	0.23	0.49	0.41	0.27	–				
JAP♂	0.53	0.44	0.43	0.61	0.60	0.84	1.12	1.36	0.73	1.32	0.49	1.61	0.06	0.67	–			
JAP♀	1.16	0.33	0.81	0.38	0.66	0.31	0.94	0.42	0.54	0.41	0.33	0.40	0.18	0.09	0.52	–		
SAM♂	1.13	0.38	0.82	0.35	0.66	0.45	1.04	0.66	0.71	0.44	0.26	0.55	0.17	0.08	0.42	0.09	–	
SAM♀	2.96	1.34	2.18	1.00	1.64	0.83	1.75	0.48	1.47	0.21	1.06	0.25	1.21	0.32	1.89	0.53	0.60	–

♂ = male; ♀ = female.

Figure 5. <u>Dendrogram of Penrose distances between</u>
<u>nine population groups subdivided by sex</u>
<u>(on the basis of four length measurements)</u>

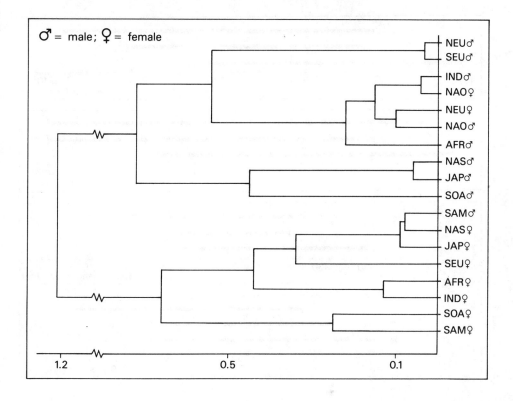

Figure 6. <u>Ranges from smallest P5 to largest P95 for</u>
<u>four length measurements of the three blocks</u>
<u>(I, II, III) in figure 5 (measurements in mm)</u>

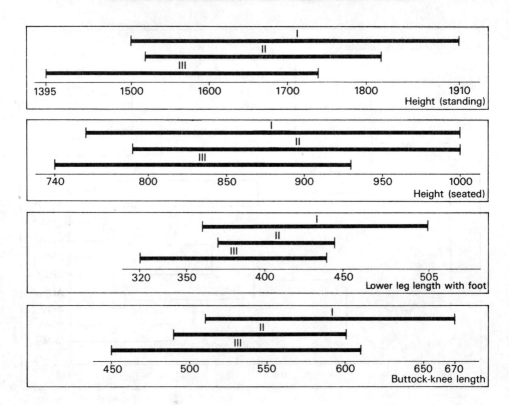

It appears from figure 6 that the block of Far Eastern male populations shown in figure 5, with the exception of P5, has a buttock-knee length which falls within the range of the first block; this is why this group has also been included in this dendrogram. There are, however, some extremely wide areas of overlap with the third block, which means that we can nevertheless identify an intermediate position. In general, the ranges for both leg measurements for the Far Eastern block show a clear proportional shift in comparison with the first block. On the basis of the dendrogram and the above considerations we come to the conclusion that the world population should be subdivided into the following two anthropometric types:

8593d

Large type	Small type
Male populations from –	Male populations from –

Northern Europe   South America
Southern Europe
Near East
India
South-East Asia
Northern Asia
Japan

Female populations from –   Female populations from –

Northern Europe   Southern Europe
Near East   Northern Asia
                            Japan
                            Africa
                            India
                            South-East Asia
                            South America

7.3 The dividing lines

Having differentiated the grouped populations on the basis of a bundle of characteristics into two basic types, plus an intermediate type which can be added to one of the other distinct groups, the question arises as to which points in the series of measurements should be taken for drawing a metrically accurate dividing line to separate one group from the other; as in many cases there are substantial areas of overlap from P95 of the smaller and P5 of the larger type.

Before we decide on a procedure, the following possibilities should be considered.

The group mean points as dividing lines. An immediately evident possibility is to establish the group mean point as $\bar{\bar{x}}$ of all mean values of all the populations, for each of the body measurements considered, and then to take the corresponding value as the dividing line. This solution, however, gives rise to the following objection. The establishment of the group mean $\bar{\bar{x}}$ corresponds to the creation of a mean value for the world population. We can then calculate the related scatter and on this basis determine P5 and P95 for each measurement. However, from the calculation of the distance measurements and the dendrogram it is known that there will be a strong expression of sexual differentiation. This means that in establishing a group mean $\bar{\bar{x}}$ we are trying to confine a bimodal subdivision into a single modal form. In consequence, we would artificially cut off the extreme values of both types, i.e. very high and very low values respectively, so that from the outset we should be

excluding those parts of the populations on the basis of whose
body dimensions it was originally considered desirable to have a
type classification. Figure 7 illustrates this effect, using the
example of stature.

Figure 7.   <u>World population, smaller type and larger
            type, with their mean values and extreme
            measurements (P5, P95, $\bar{x} \pm 2s$), using
            stature as an example</u>

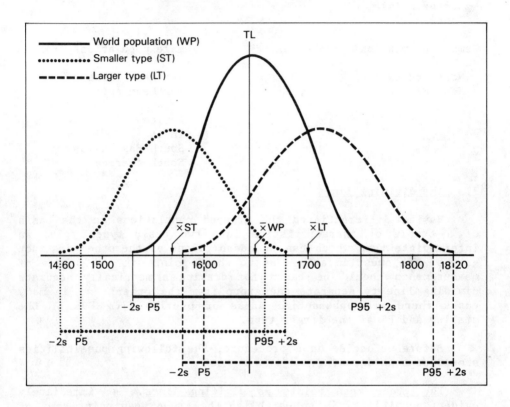

The group mean $\bar{\bar{x}}$ of the world population is 1,650 mm and the
related scatter s = 60 mm. From this we obtain the values 1,550
mm for P5 and 1,750 mm for P95. Even if we extend the range
using the formula $\bar{x} \pm 2$ s to values of 1,530 mm to 1,770 mm, this
will not cover the extremes within individual populations. In
figure 7 we have also shown the group means for the two separate
types and have taken as the dividing line the mid-point between
the group means. For the smaller type $\bar{x}_{ST}$ = 1,570 mm where s =
56 mm, and for the larger type $\bar{x}_{LT}$ = 1,700 mm where s = 62.
Correspondingly, the extreme P5 of the smaller type $P5_{ST}$ =
1,480 mm and P95 of the larger type $P95_{LT}$ = 1,805 mm. An
enlargement of the corresponding zones to $\pm$ 2 s gives for the

smaller type the extreme value of 1,460 mm and for the larger type the extreme value of 1,820 mm. Even with this range, however, some of the P95s of the large-type populations and some of the P5s of the smaller type are excluded.

The following male populations are taller than P95 of the world population (1,750 mm): North Africa, Near East, Europeans from Latin America, the Iberian Peninsula, France, South-Eastern, Eastern and Central Europe, Northern Europe, North America and Australia, Japan, North Asia, North India, West and South-Eastern Africa. If we increase the range to $\overline{\overline{x}}$ + 2 s (1,770 mm), from these 16 populations only the North Indians will be included. For the other 15 populations, the P95 for their stature will be above this figure.

The populations that are smaller than P5 (1,550 mm) are all the female populations except those from Northern and Central Europe and Australia. If we reduce this value to $\overline{\overline{x}}$ − 2 s (1,530 mm) we also include women from North America, Eastern and South-Eastern Europe, France and the Near East. All the remaining 12 female populations have a P5 stature under this value. Men from South India and South-East Asia, together with Latin American Indians, also have a P5 below that for the world population.

If we now take as a basis the group mean of the P95 for the larger type (1,805 mm) and the group mean of the P5 for the smaller type (1,480 mm), we still leave out 12 male populations (North Africa, Europeans-Negroids from Latin America, Iberian Peninsula, France, South-eastern Europe, Northern, Central and Eastern Europe, North America, Europeans from Australia, Japan and North Asia) and six female populations (Indians from Latin America, South-East Asia, South China, North and South India and West Africa). If we extend the range to that from $\overline{x}_{ST}$ − 2 s to $\overline{x}_{LT}$ + 2 s (1,460 mm–1,820 mm), this leads to no change for the female populations and for the male populations we bring in only three others, namely those from North Africa, North Asia and Japan.

The P95s of the smaller and the P5s of the larger type do not interest us for the moment, as they are in any case within the range of measurements taken into account. They can be seen in figure 7.

For the reasons explained, it appears undesirable to determine the dividing line on the basis of the group mean for the world population or on the basis of the average distance between the group means.

Consideration of the largest range (construction of type-classified populations). The explanations so far given have clearly shown that procedures which have been found adequate and satisfactory for biological descriptive purposes are not sufficient if we wish to examine, analyse and classify human populations from the ergonomic standpoint. For ergonomists it is not enough to divide populations on the basis of their mean values, as the variation in body measurements between the fifth and 95th percentiles must be taken into account not only for each individual population but also for all populations world-wide. In pursuing this objective, the only possibility is to integrate the limiting values P5 and P95 of the extreme populations in the world compilation into the ergonomic picture of the human race. Using this approach, we have put together from the world compilation the smallest P5 values and the largest P95 values respectively for each measurement individually. These two compilations of extreme values provide the limits for a new "small type" at the lower end and a new "large type" at the upper end. The dividing line between the two can appropriately be taken as half way along the range. For stature the value is 1,650 mm. We denote this value as P95 of the smaller type and at the same time P5 of the larger type. For the individual measurements we obtain the values given in table 4. This combination of measurements corresponds to a hypothetical P50 of the world population.

In a similar way, P50 of the smaller and P50 of the larger type can be determined, the range from P5 to P95 being divided in half each time. The values for P50 of the smaller and larger types are also given in table 4.

Table 4. Anthropometric classification of the world population
          into two categories: "smaller type" and "larger type"

Body measurement	Smaller type			Larger type		
	P5	P50	P95	P5	P50	P95
Stature	1 390	1 520	1 650	1 780	1 910	
Sitting height	740	800	870	935	1 000	
Eye height, sitting	620	690	750	815	880	
Forward reach (fingertips)	670	740	810	880	950	
Shoulder breadth (bideltoid)	320	365	410	455	500	
Shoulder breadth (biacromial)	285	325	360	395	430	
Hip breadth (standing)	260	300	335	375	410	
Knee height	405	455	505	550	600	
Lower leg length (popliteal height)	320	365	410	460	505	
Elbow—grip length	270	305	340	375	410	
Buttock–knee length	450	505	560	615	670	
Buttock–heel length	830	920	1 010	1 100	1 190	
Hip breadth (sitting)	260	305	350	395	440	
Hand length	140	155	170	185	200	
Hand breadth	65	75	90	100	110	
Foot length	200	225	250	275	300	
Head circumference	475	505	540	570	600	
Head length	160	175	185	195	205	
Head breadth	120	135	145	160	170	

7.4 Comparison of type-classified persons (northern and southern types) with an existing standard

The following presentation takes four measurements of body length and compares the measurements obtained with standard DIN/ISO 3411, for earth-moving machinery.

Table 5. Measurements from DIN/ISO 3411

	P5	P50	P95
Stature	1 550	1 715	1 880
Sitting height	800	880	960
Buttock-knee length	530	590	650
Lower leg length (popliteal height)	400	445	490

A comparison of these measurements from DIN/ISO 3411 with the values obtained by us on the basis of the world compilation gives the following for P95:

	P95	ISO 3411 for comparison
Stature	1 910	1 880
Sitting height	1 000	960
Buttock-knee length	670	650
Lower leg length (popliteal height)	505	490

A comparison of these two sets of data makes it clear that the upper limit contained in DIN/ISO 3411 cannot be regarded as adequate. The world compilation shows that the stature of P95 of the following male populations is not covered by the standard: France, North America, Northern Europe and Australia (Europeans). For sitting height this list also contains three further populations: Latin America (Europeans-Negroids), Central Europe and Japan.

8593d

For the lower leg length (popliteal height) the picture is as follows: North America, Northern Europe and Central Europe are not covered. For the buttock-knee length measurement North Africa, France, North America, Northern Europe, Central Europe and Australia (Europeans) are not covered.

The inadequate coverage of body measurements at the world level becomes even clearer if we look at the lower limits of P5. The values for this in DIN/ISO 3411 are as follows:

	DIN/ISO 3411	P5 for comparison
Stature	1 550	1 390
Sitting seat height	800	740
Buttock-knee length	530	450
Lower leg (popliteal height)	400	320

For the sitting height P5 of DIN/ISO 3411, at 800 mm, corresponds to P50 of the small type. For the other three measurements, P5 of DIN/ISO 3411 is greater than P50 of the small type. The differences between P5 from DIN/ISO 3411 and the small type are 30 mm for stature, 25 mm for buttock-knee length and 35 mm for lower leg length (popliteal height). The differences between P5 of DIN/ISO 3411 and P5 of the small type are 160 mm for stature, 60 mm for sitting height, 80 mm for buttock-knee length and 80 mm for lower leg length (popliteal height).

Overall, the comparison of the four length measurements shown here makes it clear that the attempt made in DIN/ISO 3411 to cover the world population by a single type classification is unsatisfactory.

7.5 The practical application of a two-type anthropometric concept

In Chapter 3 we set out the various possibilities for adapting the technical environment to the great variety of human body measurements and proportions. We identified the most important mechanisms for achieving this in practice as being, first, the adjustability of the technical elements in the human machine system and, second, the manufacture of different "sizes". Other ways of solving this problem, for example by taking account of one "critical" measurement, can be applied only in a few individual cases. The least desirable solution, that of adapting the individual to the mechanical elements by selecting specific persons and excluding others, must remain limited to exceptional cases.

The two-type concept involving a smaller and a larger type of person, as proposed here, is an attempt to combine the two major systems of adaptation, by providing for the manufacture of different (in this case two) sizes with adjustability.

The example quoted above of the earth-moving machinery operator in DIN/ISO 3411 is of course correctly based on only one "size" of product with provisions for adjustment to the body measurements of individuals from the fifth to the 95th percentiles. Our comparative survey in section 7.4 made it clear that, with the restriction resulting from this single size, a very wide range of adjustability must be provided in order to take account of differences in body measurements of earth-moving machine operators determined anthropometrically on a world-wide basis. It also became clear that the ISO concept, hitherto adopted, in spite of the available possibilities for adjustment, excludes a substantial proportion of the world population, in differing degrees from one region to another, but in particular on account of sex differences. At the present time, there is already a tendency to extend this anthropometric concept that has been used for earth-moving machine operators to other specific types of product, sometimes on the basis of the "types of person" involved. It is necessary to take action in good time to head off the resulting disadvantages, which in the foreseeable future could have a world-wide effect. This has been proposed in the present monograph, which is based on data collected and evaluated on a uniform basis.

It would be desirable to extend the range from the fifth to the 95th percentiles, taking as a starting point the body measurements of all the main populations of the earth; this, however, would involve making all the human-machine points of contact adjustable, which would be costly and not always feasible. It is therefore desirable for this "adjustment" principle to take second place to the principle of subdivision into several size ranges, which should ideally cover the respective areas of movement to which they relate. Although this two-size principle incorporates narrower ranges of body measurements, it nevertheless provides a two-type anthropometric classification, which covers all major populations of the world.

Bibliography

I. Literature referred to in the text

Backwin, H.; McLaughlin, S.D. "Increase in stature - Is the end in sight?", in The Lancet, 1964, 1195.

Barkla, D. "The estimation of body measurements of British population in relation to seat design", in Ergonomics, 4 (1961), 123.

Borkan, G.A.; Hults, D.E.; Glynn, R.J. "Role of longitudinal change and secular trend in age differences in male body dimensions", in Human Biology, 55 (1983), 629.

Büchi, E.C. "Anderungen der Körperform beim erwachsenen Menschen", in Anthropologische Forschungen, Bd. 1, Vienna, 1950.

Flugel, B.; Greil, H.; Sommer, K. Anthropologischer Atlas. Frankfurt, Edition Wötzel, 1986.

Garrett, J.W.; Kennedy, K.W. A collation of anthropometry, Aerospace Medical Research Laboratory AMRL-TR-68-1. Ohio, Wright-Patterson, 1971.

Jürgens, H.W. "Korrekturen für die Längenmessung am Unterschenkel", in Anthropologischer Anzeiger, 24 (1960a), 184.

———. "Uber die Reifung der Proportionen in der Akzeleration", in Zeitschrift für Morphologie und Anthropologie, 51 (1960b), 26.

———. "Welchen Einfluss haben akzelerationsbedingte Formveränderungen des menschlichen Körpers auf die angewandte Anthropologie, in Zentralblatt für Arbeitswissenschaft, 10 (1961), 149.

———. "Uber das Wachstum der Körpergrösse beim 'erwachsenen' Menschen", in Deutsche Medizinische Wochenschrift, 91 (1966), 1881.

———. "On body growth in adults", in Proceedings of the Eighth International Congress of Anthropology, Tokyo, 1968, Vol. I, p. 58.

———. "Anthropometric reference systems", in Schmidtke, H. Ergonomic data for equipment design. New York, Plenum, 1984, p. 93.

---; Matzdorff, I. "Spezielle industrieanthropologische Methoden", in Martin, R.; Knussmann, R. Lehrbuch der Anthropologie, Stuttgart, Fischer, 1988.

Kenntner, G. Die Veränderungen der Körpergrösse des Menschen, Ph.D. thesis, Karlsruhe, 1963.

Knussmann, R. "Penrose-Abstand und Diskriminanzanalyse", in Homo, 18 (1967), p. 134.

Kogi, K.; Sen, R.N. "Third world ergonomics", in International Revues of Ergonomics, 1 (1987), 77.

Krogman, W.M. Growth of men. Tabulae Biologicae XX, The Hague, Junk, 1941.

Lewin, T.; Jürgens, H.W. "Uber die Vergleichbarkeit von anthro-pometrischen Daten", in Zeitschrift für Morphologie und Anthropologie, 61 (1969), 33.

Martin, R. Lehrbuch der Anthropologie. Jena, Fischer, 1914; 2nd impression, 1928.

---; Saller, K. Lehrbuch der Anthropologie. Stuttgart, Fischer, 1957-66.

---; Knussmann, R. Lehrbuch der Anthropologie. Stuttgart, Fischer, 1988.

Matzdorff, I. "Women at work in workplaces designed for men", in Work and Stress, 1 (1987), 293.

---. "Social and economic consequences of an international ergonomic standardisation", in Megaw, E.D. Contemporary Ergonomics, Proceedings of the Ergonomics Society Conference, Swansea, 1987, pp. 167.

Miall, W.E. et al. "A longitudinal study of the decline of adult height with age in two Welsh communities", in Human Biology, 39 (1967), 445.

NASA. Anthropometric source book, Vol. 2, NASA Reference Publication 1024, Ohio, Yellow Springs, 1978.

Ohyama, S. et al. "Some secular changes in body height and proportion of Japanese medical students", in American Journal of Physical Anthropology, 73 (1987), 179.

Pheasant, S. "A technique for estimating anthropometric data from the parameters of the distribution of stature", in Ergonomics, 25 (1982), 981.

---. Body space. Anthropometry, ergonomics and design. London, Taylor and Francis, 1986.

Roche, A.F. "Secular trends in stature, weight and maturation", in Monographs of the Society for Research in Child Development, 44 (1979), 3.

Roebuck, J.A.; Kroemer, K.H.E.; Thomson, W.G. Engineering anthropometry methods. New York, Wiley, 1975.

Schneider, L.W. et al. Development of anthropometrically based design specifications for an advanced adult anthropometric dummy family. Washington, DC, United States Department of Transportation, 1983.

Tanner, J.M. et al. "Increase in length of leg relative to trunk in Japanese children and adults from 1957-1977", in Annals of Human Biology, 9 (1982), 411.

II. Literature drawn upon for the world compilation

Abraham, S. et al. Height and weight of adults 18-74 years of age in the United States, Advancedata No. 3, 19, United States Department of Health, Education and Welfare, Public Health Service, National Center for Health Statistics, Rockville, Maryland, Nov. 1976.

---. Weight and height of adults 18-74 years of age: United States, 1971-74, data from the National Health Survey Series 11, No. 211. Hyattsville, Maryland, National Center for Health Statistics, May 1979.

Alexander, M.; Clauser, C.E. Anthropometry of common working postures, AMRL-TR-65-73. Ohio, Wright-Patterson Air Force Base, Aerospace Medical Research Laboratories, Dec. 1965.

Anderson, W.F.; Cowan, N.R. "Body weight in older people", in Clinical Science, 29 (1965), 33-39.

Anh, Tran; Tien-Loi, Vu. "Etudes anthropologiques des Mois Rhadés", in Bulletins et Mémoires de la Société anthropologique de Paris, Séries XI, 9 (1966), 91-107.

Anthropologisches Institut Kiel. Anthropometrische Untersuchungen an Erwachsenen im nördlichen Teil der Volksrepublik China, unpublished manuscript, Kiel, 1986.

Antropometriceskij atlas. Metodiceskie rekomendacii. Moscow, 1977.

Ashbym O. Ergonomics handbook I: Human factors design data. Body size and strength. Pretoria, Design Institute, 1978.

Ashizawa, K. et al. "Anthropometrical data of Japanese female students obtained in parallel with moiré topography", in Journal of Human Ergology, 15 (1986), 167-169.

Atterhög, J.-H. et al. "Significance of primary T wave aberrations in the electrocardiogram of asymptomatic young men", in Uppsala Journal of Medical Sciences, 85 (1980), 179-191.

Austin, D.M. et al. "Work capacity and body morphology of Bantu and Pygmoid groups of Western Zaire", in Human Biology, 51 (1979), 79-89.

Bailey, D.A. et al. "Somatotypes of Canadian men and women", in Human Biology, 54 (1982), 813-828.

Balgir, R.S. "Etude morphométrique du pied des Sikligars, Penjab", in Bulletins et Mémoires de la Société anthropologique de Paris, Séries XIV, 2 (1985), 63-66.

Barancewicz, J.; Niemiec, S. "Rozwoj fizyczny mlodziezy akademickiej w wieku od 18 do 26 lat", in Biuletyn Wojskowej Akademii Medycznej (Lódz), Supp. I, 17 (1974a), 5-38.

———. "Prownanie zmian ontogenetycznych wybranych proporcjia ciala u mlodiezy w wieku 18-25 lat, badanych w latach 1956 i 1966-1970", in Biuletyn Wojskowej Akademii Medycznej (Lódz), Supp. I, 17 (1974b), 87-111.

Batogowska, A.; Slowikowski, J. Atlas antropometryczny doroslej ludnozci polski dla potrzeb projektowania. Warsaw, Instytut Wzornictwa Przemyslowego, 1974.

Beckers, R.; Pleysier, FR. "Antropometrische analyse bij de belgische dienstplichtigen. Militiejaar 1976", in Archives belges de Médecine sociale et d'Hygiène, 38 (1980), 365-416.

Berglund, L. et al. Kroppsmatt i sittande hos vuxna. Rapport baserad pa undersökningar av män och kvinnor i aldrarna 15 - 70 ar, Anatomiska Institutionen, Göteborgs Universitet och Institutionen för Trafiksäkerhet, Chalmers Tekniska Högskola, 1974.

Bernard, M.; Hueber, A. "Connaissance du pied masculin adulte", in Technicuir, 2 (1968), 136-162.

———. "Connaissance du pied féminin adulte", in Technicuir, 3 (1969), 150-178.

Bharadwaj, H. et al. "Estimation of body density and lean body weight from measurements at high altitude", in European Journal of Applied Physiology and Occupational Physiology, 36 (1977), 141-150.

Bielicki, T. et al. "The influence of three socio-economic factors on body height in Polish military conscripts", in Human Biology, 53 (1981), 543-555.

Bjelke, E. "Variation in height and weight in the Norwegian population", in British Journal of Preventive and Social Medicine, 25 (1971), 192-202.

Board of Trade. Women's measurements and sizes. London, Her Majesty's Stationery Office, 1957.

Borkan, G.A.; Norris, A.H. "Fat redistribution and the changing body dimensions of the adult male", in Human Biology, 49 (1977), 495-514.

Borkan, G.A. et al. "Role of longitudinal change and secular trend in age differences in male body dimensions", in Human Biology, 55 (1983), 629-641.

Botezatu, D. et al. "Caracteristicile antropologice ale populatiilor din satele Neagra Sarului (Tara Dornelor) si Brusturoasa (Valea superioara a trotusului)", in Studii si Cercetari de Antropologie (Bucuresti), 18 (1981), 27-33.

Bouisset, S.; Monod, H. "Un essai de détermination de caractéristiques anthropométriques en vue de l'aménagement de postes de travail: Etude de 110 cadres de la région parisienne", in Travail humain, 24 (1961), 35-50.

Bouisset, S. et al. "Mésures d'encombrement concernant de jeunes adultes français. Etude et comparaison avec des mésures anthropométriques classiques", in Bulletins et Mémoires de la Société anthropologique de Paris, Séries XI, 1 (1960), 342-350.

Brekelmans, F.E.M. et al. Anthropometric sample DUTCHMIL '85. Soesterberg, Institute for Perception TNO, Report 1986-17.

Brian, L. et al. "Apport à l'anthropométrie du pied pour des applications théoriques et pratiques", in Cahiers d'Anthropologie et Biométrie Humaine, 2, 2 (1984), 1-9.

Brian, L.; Guerci, A. "Ricerce constituzionalistica su reclute dell'Esercito Italiano", in Rivista di Antropologia, 60 (1977-79), 53-62.

Bullock, M.I.; Steinberg, M. "An anthropometric survey of Australian civilian male and female pilots", in Control, 2 (1975), 29–43.

British Standards Institution. Anthropometric and ergonomic recommendations for dimensions in designing for the elderly. BS 4467, 1969.

Carver, N. et al. "Anthropometric values for a large group of London subjects", in Proceedings, Nutrition Society, 45 (1986), A 58.

Castro e Almeida, M. de. "Da estatura, peso e sue correlacao em gentes nativas de Angola", in Revista da Juntas das Missoes Geograficas e de Investigaciones do Ultramar, 4 (1956), 485–494.

Centre d'études et de recherches d'anthropologie appliqué (CERRA). Etude anthropométrique des personnels militaires des armées. Paris, Document AA 50/73, 1973.

Centre d'études techniques des industries de l'habillement (CETIH). Nouvelles tailles masculines. Bareme 1968/69. Asteria.

Chabeuf, M. "Contribution à l'étude anthropométrique des conscrits Bourguignons", in Bulletins et Mémoires de Société anthropologique de Paris, Séries XI, 6 (1964), 443–459.

———. "Contribution à l'anthropologie des Vietnamiens méridionaux", in Bulletins et Mémoires de Société anthropologique de Paris, Séries XII, 1 (1967), 155–176.

———. "Les caractères physiques de sept populations Malgaches", in Bulletins et Mémoires de Société anthropologique de Paris, Séries XII, 4 (1969), 181–207.

Chamla, M.-C. "L'accroissement de la stature en France de 1800 à 1960; comparaison avec les pays d'Europe occidentale", in Bulletins et Mémoires de Société anthropologique de Paris, Séries XI, 6 (1964), 201–278.

Chapanis, A. (ed.). Ethnic variables in human factors engineering. Baltimore and London, Johns Hopkins University Press, 1975.

Chen, K.P. et al. "Body form, composition and some physiological functions of Chinese on Taiwan", in Annals of the New York Academy of Sciences, 110, part II (1963), 760–778.

Chmelar, J. "Antropometricke hodnoty CS. pilotu se zretelem na konstrukci jejich pracovniho stanoviste" (Anthropometric data of Czechoslovak pilots in view of their operating points arrangement), in Pracovni Lekarstvi, 19 (1967), 106–110.

Chopra, S.R.K. "A study of some morphological variables in populations living at varying altitude environments", in Proceedings of the Eighth International Congress of Anthropological and Ethnological Sciences, 1968, Tokyo and Kyoto, Vol. I, 158–162. Tokyo, Science Council of Japan, 1969.

Clarke, M.F. "The relation of weight to stature in young Indian women: Studies at two medical colleges", in Indian Journal of Medical Research, 54 (1966a), 389–401.

———. "Reference weights of young Indian women computed from stature, body girths and diameters: Studies at two medical colleges", in Indian Journal of Medical Research, 54 (1966b), 942–954.

———. "Stature and hip width of young women, students of medicine and nursing", in Human Biology, 43 (1971), 549–556.

Clauser, C. et al. "Anthropometry of Air Force women", AMRL–TR–70–5. Ohio, Wright–Patterson Air Force Base, Aeromedical Research Laboratory, Apr. 1972.

Clements, E.M.B.; Pickett, K.G. "Stature and weight of men from England and Wales in 1941", in British Journal of Preventive and Social Medicine, 11 (1957), 51–60.

Corrain, C. "Caratteri morfometrico e constituzionali di un gruppo di detenuti nella Casa Penale di Padova", in Medicina Legale e delle Assicurazione, Vol. IV, Fasc. 4, 1956.

———. "Ricerche antropometriche nel Gargano", in Memorie di Biogeografia Adriatica, Vol. IV, Padua, Tipografia del Seminario, 1962.

———. "Saggio antropologico sulla popolazione di Chioggia (Venezia)", in Rivista di Antropologia, 52 (1965), 177–181.

———. Antropologia della Lessinia, Memorie del museo civico di storia naturale. Verona, 1976.

Corrain, C. et al. "Caratteri morfometrici in un gruppo di militari di reclutamento alpino delle Venezie", in Gornale di Medicina Militare, 112 (1962), 599–611.

---. Ricerche antropologiche sulla popolazione dei Colli
Euganei. Padua, Società Cooperativa Tipografica, 1969.

---. "Alcune ricerche antropologiche tra le popolazioni
dell'alta Valle del Fersina (Trento)", in Studi Trentini di
Scienze Naturali, 50, 2 (1973), 141-172.

---. "Caratteri antropometrici tra i Ladini dell'Alto Cordevole
(Belluno)", in Studi Trentini di Scienze Naturali, 51, N. 1
B (1974), 137-155.

Correnti, V. "L'accrescimento da 6 a 20 anni nella popolazione
palermitana - Ricerche longitudinal a breve termine", in
Rivista di Antropologia, Supp. 55 (1969).

Correnti, V. et al. "Indagine antropologica 1970 nel basso
Dahomey. Nota I - Caratteri morfologici e morfometrici
degli adulti", in Rivista di Antropologia, 58 (1972-73),
39-76.

Courtney, A.J. "Hand anthropometry of Hong Kong Chinese females
compared to other ethnic groups", in Ergonomics, 27 (1984),
1169-1180.

---; Ng, M.K. "Hong Kong female hand dimensions and machine
guarding", in Ergonomics, 27 (1984), 187-193.

Création de modèles tridimensionelles de pilotes d'avions
militaires. Doc. A.A. 160/84. Paris, Anthropologie
Appliqué, Oct. 1984.

Cresta, M. "Recherches biologiques, nutritionelles et sanitaires
sur des populations de la République Populaire du Congo et
problèmes liés au développement rural. IV. Anthropologie
morphologique de certains groupes de population des
districts de Ewo et de Kindama", in Rivista di Antropologia,
63 (1985), 61-76.

Cristescu, M. et al. "Aspects de la variabilité de la stature en
Roumanie", in Studii si Cercetari de Antropologie
(Bucuresti), 15 (1978), 17-21.

Cullumbine, H. et al. "Influence of age, sex physique and
muscular development on physical fitness", in Journal of
Applied Physiology, 2 (1950), 488-511.

Cvicelova, M. "Les forces maxima de soulèvement des femmes non
sportives et de celles pratiquant sport d'une façon active",
in Acta Facultatis Rerum Naturalium Universitatis
Comenianae, Anthropologia, 30-31 (1982-83), 1-11.

8593d

Damon, A. "Negro-white differences in pulmonary function (vital capacity, timed vital capacity, and expiration flow rate)", in Human Biology, 38 (1966), 380-393.

---; Thomas, R.B. "Fertility and physique - height, weight, and ponderal index", in Human Biology, 39 (1967), 5-13.

Danmarks Statistik "Tabel 46. Sessionsresultaterne og de värnepligtiges höyde", in Statistisk Arbog, 88 (1984), 48.

Das, B.M. et al. "Anthropological studies in Assam, India. 1. Observations on five Mongoloid populations", in Anthropologischer Anzeiger, 43 (1985a), 193-204.

---. "Anthropological studies in Assam, India. 2. Observations on Muslims", in Anthropologischer Anzeiger, 43 (1985b), 299-310.

---. "Anthropological studies in Assam, India. 3. Observations on three Brahmin groups", in Anthropologischer Anzeiger, 44 (1986a), 35-43.

---. "Anthropological studies in Assam, India. 4. Observations on the Kalitas", in Anthropologischer Anzeiger, 44 (1986b), 105-115.

---. "Anthropological studies in Assam, India. 5. Observations on four further groups (Jogis, Hiras, Kumars, Kaibartas)", in Anthropologischer Anzeiger, 44 (1986c), 239-248.

Davies, B.T. et al. "Female hand dimensions and guarding of machines", in Ergonomics, 23 (1980a), 79-84.

---. "A comparison of hand enthropometry of females in three ethnic groups", in Ergonomics, 23 (1980b), 179-182.

Davies, C.T.M. et al. "Exercise tolerance and body composition of male and female Africans aged 18-30 years", in Human Biology, 45 (1973), 31-40.

Debetz, G.J. "Recherches anthropologiques en Afghanistan", in Proceedings of the Eighth International Congress of Anthropological and Ethnological Sciences, 1968, Tokyo and Kyoto, Vol. I, 139-143. Tokyo, Science Council of Japan, 1969.

Dellaportas, G.J. "Growth of schoolchildren in Gondar area, Ethiopia", in Human Biology, 41 (1969), 218-222.

Delwaide, P.A. et al. "Corrélations entre divers paramètres anthropométriques, l'eau corporelle et le potassium total", in Biométrie Humaine, 8 (1973), 39–51.

Department of Defense (ed.). Military handbook. Anthropometry of US military personnel (metric). Department of Defense, DOD-HDBK-743 (METRIC), 3 Oct. 1980.

Deutsches Institut für Normung. Körpermasse des Menschen. Werte, DIN 33 402, Part 2, 1979.

Diaz Ungria, A.G. de et al. "Biotipologia y medicina social", in Los Guarao del Delta Amacuro, Caracas, Universidad Central de Venezuela, Departemento de Sociologia y Antropologia Cultural, 1956.

Dobon, L.C. "Carácteres antropológicos de la población Leonesa", in Antropología de España y América (Madrid) (1977), 109–118.

Duggal, N.; Nath, S. "Estimation of stature using percutaneous length of radius, ulna and tibia among Lodhas and Mundas of district Midnapore, West Bengal", in Anthropologie (Brno), 24 (1986), 23–27.

Durnin, J.V.G.A.; Womersley, J. "Body fat assessed from total body density and its estimation from skinfold thickness: Measurements on 481 men and women aged 16–72 years", in British Journal of Nutrition, 32 (1974), 77–97.

Ente Italiano della Moda. Le misure antropometriche della popolazione Italiana. L'abbigliamento delle classi giovani dai 6 ai 19 anni. Milan, Franco Angeli, 1979.

Erishman, F.F. "The physical development of factory workers of Central Rumania", in Izbrannye proizvedenija, Moscow, Selected Works, Vol. 2, 1959, 208–250.

Estryn, M. et al. "Etude anthropométrique du personnel féminin des hôpitaux de Paris. Intérêt dans la conception des postes de travail", in Travail Humain, 39 (1976), 285–298.

Eveleth, P.B. "An anthropometric study of Northeastern Brazilians", in American Journal of Physical Anthropology, 37 (1972), 223–232.

Finger, G.; Harbeck, R. "Uber einige morphologische Daten 20 jähriger Männer", in Homo, 12 (1961), 65–107.

Floris, G. et al. "Costituzioni ed altimetria in Sardegna", in Archivio di Antropologia et di Etnologia, 116 (1986), 167–173.

Flügel, B. et al. Anthropologischer Atlas: Alters- und Geschlechtsvariabilität des Menschen: Grundlagen und Daten. Frankfurt am Main. Edition Wötzel, 1986.

Friedlaender, J. et al. "Longitudinal physique changes among healthy white veterans at Boston", in Human Biology, 49 (1977), 541-558.

Frisancho, R.A. et al. "Pattern of growth of lowland and highland Peruvian Quechua of similar genetic composition", in Human Biology, 47 (1975), 233-243.

Garrett, J.W. Anthropometry of the hands of male Air Force flight personnel, AMRL-TR-69-42. Ohio, Wright-Patterson Air Force Base, Aerospace Medical Research Laboratory, Mar. 1970.

---; Kennedy, K.W. A collation of anthropometry, AMRL-TR-68-1, Vols. I and II. Ohio, Wright-Patterson Air Force Base, Aerospace Medical Research Laboratory, Mar. 1971.

Gavrilovic, Z.; Badojevic, P. "Some anthropometric data about children and youth of Vrsac obtained by examination in 1981 and 1982", Zbornik radova privodno-matematicki fakultet Novi Sad, serya biologigu, 14 (1984), 5-11.

Gessain, M. "Implications anthropologiques de l'évolution des Bassari du Sénégal oriental depuis 1900", in Bulletins et Mémoires de la Société anthropologique de Paris, 6, Séries XIII (1979), 389-397.

Glanville, E.V.; Geerdink, R.A. "Skinfold thickness, body measurements and age changes in Trio and Wajana Indians of Surinam", in American Journal of Physical Anthropology, 32 (1970), 455-462.

Gomez, P.G. "Estudio morfotipológico de los Asturianos del S.E., similitudes y diferencias con los Santanderinos de la Liebana", in Publicaciones del Instituto de Etnografía y Folklore, "Hoyos Sainz", 8 (1977-78), 89-112.

---. "Esbozo morfotipológico de la población de Liebana", in Publicaciones del Instituto de Etnografía y Folklore, "Hoyos Sainz", 9 (1976), 213-249.

Gorny, S. "Zdjecie antropometryczne Polski Czesc I. Pomiary ludnosci doroslej z lat 1955-1956" [Anthropometric Survey of Poland, Part I, measurement of adults, 1955-1956], in Materialy i Prace Antropologiczne, No. 84, 1972.

Grandjean, E.; Burandt, U. "Körpermasse der Belegschaft eines schweizerischen Industriebetriebes", in Industrielle Organisation, 31 (1962), 239-242.

Grunhofer, H.J.; Kroh, G. (eds.). A review of anthropometric
data of German Air Force and United States Air Force flying
personnel 1967-1968, AGARDograph No. 205, Neuilly sur Seine,
NATO, AGARD, 1975.

Guerci, A. "Contributo alla conoscenza della dinamica constituzionalistica della populazione Italiana. Studio diacronica
sull'incremento staturale dei giovani in età di leva dal
1879 al 1969", in Archivio per l'Antropologia e la
Etnologia, 107 (1977), 305-315.

Gusinde, M. "The Yupa Indians in Western Venezuela", in Proceedings of the American Philosophical Society, 100 (1956),
197-222.

Halberstein, R.A.; Davies, J.E. "Biosocial aspects of high
blood pressure in people of the Bahamas, in Human Biology,
56 (1984), 317-328.

Hamill, P.V.V. et al. Body weight, stature, and sitting height:
White and Negro youths 12-17 years, United States. Vital
and Health Statistics from the National Health Survey,
Series 11, No. 126, Aug. 1973.

Hanna, J.M.; Baker, P.T. "Biocultural correlates to the blood
pressure of Samoan migrants in Hawaii", in Human Biology, 51
(1979), 481-497.

Harrison, J.M.; Marshall, W.A. "Normal standards for the
relationships between the lengths of limbs and of limb
segments in young British women: A photogrammetric study",
in Human Biology, 42 (1970), 90-104.

Haslegrave, C.M. "An anthropometric survey of British drivers",
in Ergonomics, 22 (1979), 145-153.

---. "Anthropometric profile of the British car driver", in
Ergonomics, 23 (1980), 437-467.

Hass, J. et al. "Altitude, ethnic and sex difference in birth
weight and length in Bolivia", in Human Biology, 52 (1980),
459-477.

Hauser, G.; Wytek, R. "Somatovariants of females from Northern
India", in Anthropologischer Anzeiger, 41 (1983), 129-135.

Heeneberg, M. et al. "Head size, body size, and intelligence:
Intraspecific correlations in Homo sapiens sapiens", in
Homo, 36 (1985), 207-218.

Heimendinger, J. "Die Ergebnisse von Körpermessungen an 5000 Basler Kindern von 2-18 Jahren", in Helvetica Paediatrica Acta, Supp. XIII, Vol. 19 (1964), 5.

Hertzberg, H.T.E. et al. Anthropometry of flying personnel - 1950, WADC Technical Report 52-321. Ohio, Wright Patterson Air Force Base, Wright Air Development Center, Sep. 1954.

---. Anthropometric survey of Turkey, Greece and Italy, AGARDograph 73. Oxford; London; New York; Paris, Pergamon Press, 1963.

Heyters, C. "Contribution à l'établissement de normes anthropométriques: Mensurations d'étudiants belges", in Cahiers d'Anthropologie et Biométrie Humaine, 1 (1983), 13-24.

Hiba, J.C.; Luco, M.F. de. Relevamiento antropométrico de población Argentina. Datos correspondientes a 11 variables antropométricas de varones y mujeres adultos, Rosario, Argentina, Publicacion del Departamento de Diseño Industrial, 6/82.

Hiernaux, J. "Analyse de la variation des caractères physiques humaines en une région de l'Afrique Centrale: Ruanda-Urundi et Kivu", in Annales du Musée royal du Congo belge, Anthropologie, 3 (1956).

---. "Luba du Katanga et Luba du Kasai (Congo); Comparaison de deux populations de même origine", in Bulletins et Mémoires de la Société anthropologique de Paris, Séries XI, 6 (1964), 611-622.

---. "Note sur les Tutsi de l'Itombwe (République du Congo): La position anthropologique d'une population émigrée", in Bulletins et Mémoires de la Société Anthropologique de Paris, Séries X, 7 (1965), 361-379.

Huard, P. et al. "Les enquêtes anthropologiques faites en Indochine et plus particulièrement au Vietnam", in Bulletins et Mémoires de la Société Anthropologique de Paris, Séries XI, 3 (1962), 372-438.

Hughes, J.G.; Lomaev, O. "An anthropometric survey of Australian male facial sizes", in American Industrial Hygiene Association Journal, 33 (1972), 71-78.

Huizinga, J. "New physical anthropological evidence bearing on the relationships between Dogon, Kurumba and the extinct West African Tellem population", in Proceedings Koninklijke Nederlandsche Akademie van Wetenschappen, Series C: Biological Medical Sciences, Vol. LXXI (1968), 16-30.

Ikeda, J. "Contributions to the anthropology of Iraq", in Acta Medica et Biologica, 8 (1960), 109-129.

Imabayashi, M.; Kanda, S. "Anthropolog:cal study of inhabitants in Oguni area of Yamagata prefecture", in Anthropological Reports, 38 (1982), 21-32.

---. "An anthropological study of the inhabitants in Iwate prefecture", in Anthropological Reports, 39 (1983), 49-72.

---. Anthropological study of inhabitants in Towada of Akita prefecture", in Anthropological Reports, 41 (1984a), 69-83.

---. Anthropological study of inhabitants in Ani area of Akita prefecture", in Anthropological Reports, 41 (1984b), 47-59.

Imabayashi, M.; Watanabe, T. "Anthropological study of inhabitants in Southern part of Akita prefecture", in Anthropological Reports, 41 (1984), 9-30.

Imabayashi, M. et al. "Anthropological study of inhabitants in Nakaniida of Miyagi prefecture", in Anthropological Reports, 38 (1982), 33-44.

---. "Anthropological study of inhabitants in Miomote and Niigata prefecture", in Anthropological Reports, 41 (1984), 31-46.

Ince, N.E. et al. Anthropometry of 500 Royal Armoured Corps servicemen 1972, Report APRE 36/73, Army Personnel Research Establishment, 1973.

Ingelmark, E.; Lewin, T. "Anthropometric studies on Swedish women", in Acta Morphologica Neerlando-Scandinavica, 7 (1968), 145-166.

Institut für Wehrmedizinalstatistik und Berichtswesen. "Körpermasse bei Musterungs- und Annahmeuntersuchungen 1957-72", in Beiträge zur Wehrmedizinalstatistik, 33, 1975.

Jürgens, H.W.; Pieper, U. Anthropometrische Daten von ausländischen Arbeitnehmern, Bundesanstalt für Arbeitsschutz, Dortmund. Forschungsbericht No. 373. Bremerhaven, Wirtschaftsverlag NW, 1984.

Kadanov, D.; Pandova, B. "Form und Grösse der Hand der Bulgarin", in Comptes Rendus de l'Académie Bulgare des Sciences, 20 (1967), 1225-1228.

Kadanov, D.; Mutafov, S. "Der Korrelationsgrad zwischen Körpermassen bei Erwachsenen beider Geschlechter", in Comptes Rendus de l'Académie Bulgare des Sciences, 20 (1967a), 859-862.

---. "Körperproportionen bei Bulgaren und Bulgarinnen von verschiedenem Wuchs", in Comptes Rendus de l'Académie Bulgare des Sciences, 20 (1967b), 987-999.

---. Antropologiceska standartizacija na chodilata na bulgarskoto naseleni, Sofia, Bulgarska Akademija na Naukite. Institut po Morfologija, Sekcija po Antropologija i Anatomija, 1977.

Kadanov, D. et al. Tables about body dimensions, proportions and indices of Bulgarian children and adolescents from 3 to 18 years of age of different and same height, Sofia, Bulgarska Akademija na Naukite, Institut po Morfologija, 1979.

Kanda, S. "Anthropometry of the Pathans and Kashmirian in West Pakistan. Part 1", in Medical Journal, Osaka University, 16 (1966), 235-243.

Karpinos, B.D. "Current height and weight of youths of military age", in Human Biology, 33 (1961), 335-354.

Keller, W.; Kopf, H. "Anthropometrische Daten ostafrikanischer Arbeiter im Vergleich zu Daten westdeutscher junger Männer", in Nutritio et Dieta, 5 (1963), 224-234.

Kimura, K. "Studies on growth and development in Japan", in Yearbook of Physical Anthropology, 27 (1984), 179-214.

---; Tsai, C. "Comparative studies of the physical growth in Formosans. I: Height and weight", in Journal of Anthropological Society of Nippon, 75 (1967), 11-18.

---. "Comparative studies of the physical growth in Formosans. II: Biacromial breadth and bicristal diameter", in Journal of Anthropological Society of Nippon, 76 (1968), 193-204.

Knapik, J.J. et al. "Height, weight, per cent body fat, and indices of adiposity for young men and women entering the US Army", in Aviation, Space, and Environmental Medicine, 54 (1983), 223-231.

Knussmann, R.; Knussmann, E. "Die Dama - eine Altschicht in Süd-westafrika?", in Journal der Südwest-Afrikanischen Wissen-schaftlichen Gesellschaft, 24 (1969-70), 9-32.

Koh, E.T. "Selected anthropometric measurements for low-income, black population in Mississippi", in American Dietetic Association Journal, 79 (1981), 555-561.

Kopczynski, J. "Height and weight of adults in Cracow. IV. Weight by social status and migration category", in Epidemiological Review, 16 (1972a), 465-476.

---. "Height and weight of an adult Cracow population", in Epidemiological Review, 26 (1972b), 251-262.

Krukoff, S. "Comparaisons de dimorphismes sexuels chez les Tonkinoises et chez les Françaises", in Bulletins et Mémoires de la Société anthropologique de Paris, Séries XI, 9 (1966), 165-170.

Kurth, G.; Lam, T.H. "Körperwuchsformen und Arbeitsmittel Angewandte Anthropometrie bei der Entwicklungshilfe", in Homo, 20 (1969), 209-221.

Kuyp, E. van der. "Body weights and heights of the Surinam people", in Voeding, 28 (1967), 435-469.

Kvasnicka, E.; Radl, G. Anthropometrische Erhebungen zur ergonomischen und sicherheitsgerechten Gestaltung der Arbeitsumwelt von über 40 jährigen Männern. Cologne, Technischer Überwachungsverein Rheinland, Institut für Unfallforschung. Abschlussbericht zu Forschungsvorhaben IIIb 8-3765.21 BA-2695/75. TÜV Auftrags-Nr. 400028, 1977.

Laska-Mierzejewska, T. "Desarrollo y maduración de los niños y jovenes habaneros", in Materialy i Prace Antropologiczne, 74 (1967), 9-63.

---. "Morphological and developmental difference between negro and white Cuban youths", in Human Biology, 42 (1970), 581-597.

Lasker, G.W. "Differences in anthropometric measurements within and between three communities in Peru", in Human Biology, 34 (1962), 63-70.

---; Thomas, R. "Relationship between reproductive fitness and anthropometric dimensions in a Mexican population", in Human Biology, 48 (1976), 775-791.

Latham, M.C. et al. "A comparative study of the nutritional status, parasitic infections and health of male roadworkers in four areas of Kenya", in Royal Society of Tropical Medicine and Hygiene Transactions, 76 (1982), 734-740.

Leatherman, T.L. et al. "Anthropometric survey of high-altitude Bolivian porters", in Annals of Human Biology, 11 (1984), 253-256.

Lee, J. et al. "Relative merits of the weight-corrected-for-height indices", in American Journal of Clinical Nutrition, 34 (1981), 2521-2529.

Lee, S.D. "A study of the differences and characteristics between the nations, in the measured values of the human body and the working area", in International Journal of Production Research, 16 (1978), 335-347.

Lehmann, H.; Marquer, P. "Etude anthropologique des Indiens du groupe 'Guambiano-Kokonuko' (Région de Popayàn, Colombie)", in Bulletins et Mémoires de la Société anthropologique de Paris, t. 1, Séries XI (1960), 177-237.

Lestrange, M. de. "Contribution à l'étude de l'anthropologie des Noirs d'AOF. II. Anthropométrie de 1023 Coniagui, Bassari, Badyarnké et Fulakunda de Guinée française", in Bulletins et Mémoires de la Société anthropologique de Paris, Séries X, 1 (1950), 99-136.

Lestrange, M.-Th. "Alimentation et anthropobiologie: Données concernant les Bassari, Boin et Peul de la région de Kédougou (Sénégal Oriental)", in Bulletins et Mémoires de Paris, Séries XIII, 4 (1977), 371-381.

Lewin, T. "Anthropometric studies on Swedish industrial workers when standing and sitting", in Ergonomics, 12 (1969), 883-902.

---; Skrobak-Kaczynski, J. "Anthropometrical studies on mature Swedish industrial employees", in Zeitschrift für Morphologie und Anthropologie, 64 (1972), 348-361.

Little, B.B.; Malina, R.M. "Gene flow and variation in stature and craniofacial dimensions among indigenous populations of Southern Mexico, Guatemala and Honduras", in American Journal of Physical Anthropology, 70 (1986), 505-512.

Little, J.A. et al. "Customary diet, anthropometry, and dysli-proteinemia in selected North American populations", in Lipid Research Clinics Program Prevalence Study, Circulation 73 (supp. I) (1986), 1-80.

Locati, G. et al. "Primi resultati del rilevamento di parametri antropometrici su un campione di lavoratori italiani ai fini della progettazione ergonomica del posto di lavoro", in Medicina del Lavora, 68, N. 1 (1977).

Lourie, J.A.; Taufa, T. "The Ok Tedi health and nutrition project, Papua New Guinea: Physique, growth and nutritional status of the Wopkaimin of the Star Mountains", in Annals of Human Biology, 13 (1986), 517-536.

Maksud, M.G. et al. "The aerobic power of several groups of laborers in Colombia and the United States", in European Journal of Applied Physiology and Occupational Physiology, 35 (1976), 173-182.

Malina, R.M. et al. "Ethnic and social class differences in selected anthropometric characteristics of Mexican American and Anglo adults: The San Antonio heart study", in Human Biology, 55 (1983), 867-883.

Marotta, M. La statura ed il livello mentale delle reclute sarde, Atti della XLV Riunione della Società Italiana per il Progresso delle Science, Naples. Rome, 1954.

Marquer, P.; Chamla, M.-C. "L'évolution des caractères morphologiques en fonction de l'âge, chez 2089 Français, de 20 à 91 ans", in Bulletins et Mémoires de la Société Anthropologique de Paris, Séries XI, 2 (1961), 1-78.

Martorell, R. et al. "Maternal stature, fertility and infant mortality", in Human Biology, 53 (1981), 303-312.

Martuzzi, F. "L'accrescimento post-puberale: osservazioni su un gruppo di studentesse Emiliano-Romagnole", in Endocrinologia e Scienza della Costituzione, Bologna, Vol. XXX, Part VI, 1968.

Masali, M. "Applied anthropometry in ergonomics", in Collegium Antropologicum, 1 (1977), 83-92.

Mavalwala, J. "An anthropometric survey of the Parsi community in India", in Homo, 17 (1966), 97-111.

Maxia, C.; Fenu, A. "Sulla compositizione raziale della popolazione sarda. Nota I: Comparazione antropometrica in una popolazione del Goceano (Bono) dalla fine del XVI sec. al XX sec.", in Rendiconti del Seminario della Facoltá di Scienze della Universitá di Cagliari, Padua, Vol. XXXIII, 1963a.

---. "Sulla compositizione raziale della popolazione sarda. Nota II: Studio antropometrico in una popolazione adulta di un comune della Valle Media del Tirso (Ghilarza) nello scorcio di tempo dal XIX al XX secolo", in Rendiconti del Seminario della Facoltá di Scienze della Universitá di Cagliari, Padua, Vol. XXXIII, 1963b.

---.   "Sulla compositizione raziale della popolazione sarda. Nota III: Osservazioni sulla popolazione di due comuni della Bargagia di Seulo (Seui e Seulo)", in Rendiconti del Seminario della Facoltá di Scienze della Universitá di Cagliari, Padua, Vol. XXXVII, 1967.

McConnel, W. et al. "Medical and clinical assessment of lactating women and their infants in Katmandu Valley, Nepal", in Federation Proceedings, Federation of American Societies for Experimental Biology, Baltimore, 44 (1985), 1504.

McGarvey, S.T.; Baker, P.T. "The effects of modernization and migration on Samoan blood pressures", in Human Biology, 51 (1979), 461-479.

Mendez, J.; Behrhorst, C. "The anthropometric characteristics of Indian and urban Guatemalans", in Human Biology, 35 (1963), 457-469.

Metodiceskie rekomendacii po ispozovaniju antropometricskich dannyju pri konstruirovanii proizvodstvennogo oborudovanija. Moscow, 1982.

Miall, W.E. et al. "A longitudinal study of the decline of adult height with age in two Welsh communities", in Human Biology, 39 (1967), 445-454.

Miyashita, T.; Takahashi, E. "Stature and nose height of Japanese", in Human Biology, 43 (1971), 327-339.

Molenbroek, J.M. et al. Bejaarden antropometrie. Onderzoek naar en toepassingen van afmetingen van Nederlandse bejaarden. Delft, Technische Hogeschool Delft, Tussenafdeling Industrieel Ontwerpen, 1983.

Monod, H.; Wisner, A. "Etude anthropométrique de 100 laborantines et secrétaires de la région Parisienne en vue d'applications ergonomiques", in Travail Humain, 27 (1964), 37-52.

Mooij, D. Anthropometric data for students in Iran, Occasional Papers - School Building No. 16, Colombo, Asian Regional Institute for School Building Research, 1972.

Morant, G.M. Surveys of the heights and weights of Royal Air Force personnel, FPRC 711. Farnborough, Hampshire, Flying Personnel Research Committee, RAF, Institute of Aviation Medicine, Oct. 1956.

---.; Ruffell Smith, H.P. Body measurements of pilots and cockpit dimensions, FPRC 689. Farnborough, Hampshire, Flying Personnel Research Committee, RAF, Institute of Aviation Medicine, Dec. 1947.

Morant, G.M. et al. A survey of measurement of feet and footwear of Royal Air Force personnel, FPRC 761. Farnborough, Hampshire, Flying Personnel Research Committee, RAF, Institute of Aviation Medicine, July 1952.

Morimoto, T. "An anthropological study on the Okayama prefecture", in Anthropological Reports, 43 (1986), 33-54.

---; Kanda, S. "Anthropological study of the Kanzai inhabitants in Kibi district, Okayama prefecture", in Anthropological Reports, 39 (1983), 73-82.

Morimoto, T. et al. "Anthropological study of the inhabitants in Kamabuchi of Yamagata prefecture", in Anthropological Reports, 38 (1982), 45.

Morita, S.; Ohtsuki, F. "Secular changes of the main head dimensions in Japanese", in Human Biology, 45 (1973), 151-165.

Morrison, J.F. "Design of machinery and protective equipment to take account of static and dynamic anthropometrical measurements", in South African Mechanical Engineer, May 1965, 230-233.

Morrison, J.F. et al. "An anthropometrical survey of Bantu mine labourers", in South African Institute of Mining and Metallurgy (1968), 275-279.

Moustafa, A.W. et al. "Anthropometric study of Egyptian women", in Ergonomics, 30 (1987), 1089-1098.

Mueller, W.H. et al. "The Aymara of Western Bolivia: V. Growth and development in an hypoxic environment", in Human Biology, 52 (1980), 529-546.

Mustakallio, M.; Telkkä, A. "Anthropologische Untersuchung von Bewohnern Süd-Ostbottniens", in Annales Academiae Scientificae Fennicae, A. V. 24, 1951.

Nagamine, S.; Suzuki, S. "Anthropometry and body composition of Japanese young men and women", in Human Biology, 36 (1964), 8-15.

Nakata, S. "An anthropological study of the Yamis in the Ranyu Island, Taiwan", in Anthropological Reports, 44 (1987a), 67-83.

8593d

---. "An anthropological study on the Okinawa Japanese", in Anthropological Reports, 44 (1987b), 129-153.

---; Kanda, S. "An anthropological study on the adult inhabitants of the Ikema Island", in Anthropological Reports, 44 (1987), 85-94.

Nakata, S. et al. "An anthropological study on the inhabitants of the Ie Island in Okinawa prefecture", in Anthropological Reports, 42 (1985), 83-93.

---. "An anthropological study of the inhabitants of the Tamara Island in Okinawa prefecture", in Anthropological Reports, 43 (1986), 55-65.

---. "An anthropological study of the inhabitants of the Hateruma Island in Okinawa prefecture", in Anthropological Reports, 44 (1987), 55-66.

Neves, W.A. et al. "Principal-components analysis of Brazilian Indian anthropometric data", in American Journal of Physical Anthropology, 67 (1985), 13-17.

Noppa, H. et al. "Body composition in middle-aged women with special reference to the correlation between body fat mass and anthropometric data" in American Journal of Clinical Nutrition, 32 (1979), 1388-1395.

---. "Longitudinal studies of anthropometric data and body composition. The population study of women in Göteborg, Sweden", in American Journal of Clinical Nutrition, 33 (1980), 155-162.

Nordgren, B. "Anthropometric measures and muscle strength in young women", in Scandinavian Journal of Rehabilitation Medicine, 4 (1972), 165-169.

Norges Offisielle Statistikk. "Tabell 75. Vernepliktige etter höyde. Prosent", in Statistisk Arbok, 103 (1984a), 81.

---. "Tabell 76. Gjennomsnittshöyde og svömmeferdighet for vernepliktige", in Statistisk Arbok, 103 (1984b), 81.

Novak, L.P. "Comparative study of body composition of American and Filipino women", in Human Biology, 42 (1970), 206-216.

Nowak, E. "Okreslenie przestrzeni pracy konczyn gornych dla potrzeb projektowania stanowisk roboczych", in Prace y Materialy Instytutu Wzornictwa Przemyslowego, 30 (1976).

Nurse, G.T. The body size of rural and peri-urban adult males from Lilongwe district, Malawi, Paper presented at the International Biological Program IBP/HA, Blantyre, Malawi, 5-12 April 1971.

Nylind, B. et al. "Changes in male exercise performance and anthropometric variables between the ages of 19 and 30", in European Journal of Applied Physiology and Occupational Physiology, 38 (1978), 145-150.

Ohyama, S. et al. "Some secular changes in body height and proportion of Japanese medical students", in American Journal of Physical Anthropology, 73 (1987), 179-183.

Olivier, G. Les populations du Cambodge. Paris, Masson, 1956.

---. "Révision des données sur la stature et la corpulence en France", in Bulletins et Mémoires de la Société anthropologique de Paris, Séries XIII, 2 (1975), 163-177.

---; Devigne, G. "Données nouvelles sur la stature et la corpulence en France", in Cahiers d'Anthropologie et Biométrie humaine, 3 (1985), 111-123.

Olivier, G. et al. "Documents anthropométriques sur les conscrits du Nord de la France", in Bulletins et Mémoires de la Société anthropologique de Paris, Séries X, 8 (1957), 47-60.

---. "L'accroissement de la stature en France. I. l'accélération du phénomène", in Bulletins et Mémoires de la Société anthropologique de Paris, Séries XIII, 4 (1977a), 197-204.

---. "L'accroissement de la stature en France. II. Les causes du phénomène: analyse univariée", in Bulletins et Mémoires de la Société anthropologique de Paris, Séries XIII, 4 (1977b), 205-214.

Palacios Mateos, J.M. et al. "Talla de las mujeres de Madrid en los años 1975 a 1977", in Revista Clinica Española, 151 (1978), 217-218.

Palomino, H. et al. "Altitude, hereditary and body proportions in Northern Chile", in American Journal of Physical Anthropology, 50 (1979), 39-50.

Papai, J. "Variations of physique in female college students", in Anthropologiai Kozlemenyek, 24 (1980), 173-178.

8593d

Parizkova, J.; Buzkova, P. "Relationship between skinfold thickness measured by Harpenden Caliper and densitometric analysis of total body fat in men", in Human Biology, 43 (1971), 16-21.

---; Eiselt, E. "Body composition and anthropometric indicators in old age and the influence of physical exercise", in Human Biology, 38 (1966), 351-363.

---. "A further study on changes in somatic characteristics and body composition of old men followed longitudinally for 8-10 years", in Human Biology, 43 (1971), 318-326.

---. "Longitudinal changes in body build and skinfold in a group of old men over a 16-year period", in Human Biology, 52 (1980), 803-809.

Peters, W.-H. et al. "A preliminary anthropometric study (body weight, body height, body-mass index) of Ethiopian schoolchildren and college students", in Nahrung, 31 (1987), 145-148.

Pheasant, S. Bodyspace. London and Philadelphia, Taylor and Francis, 1986.

Picon-Reategui, E. et al. "Anthropometric characteristics and body composition of Ainu and other Japanese: Comparison with other racial groups", in American Journal of Physical Anthropology, 50 (1979), 393-400.

Pisl, Z. et al. "Neke antropometrijske karakteristike stanovnistva SR Hrvatske u dobi izmedu 22. i 41. godine zivota", in Acta Medica Jugoslavica, 34 (1980), 19-28.

Pollitzer, W.S. et al. "Physical anthropology of the Negroes of Charleston, S.C.", in Human Biology, 42 (1970), 265-279.

---. "Characteristics of a population sample of Jacobina, Bahia, Brazil", in Human Biology, 54 (1982), 697-707.

Pollock, M.L. et al. "Prediction of body density in young and middle-aged women", in Journal of Applied Physiology, 38 (1975), 745-749.

Polska Akademia Nauk, Komisja Antropometrii (ed.). Zdjecie antropologiczne w latach 1955-1959 i jego zastosowania w przemysle odziezowym. Warsaw and Wroclaw, Panstwowe Wydawnictwo Naukowe (1962), 180-212.

Pomerance, H.H.; Krall, J.M. "The relationship of adult height and weight to the velocity of growth in infancy and childhood", in Human Biology, 57 (1985), 599-610.

Prokopec, M. "Dimensional characteristics of men and women in Czechoslovakia for the purposes of industry", in Ergonomics in Machine Design, Vol. I. Occupational Safety and Health Series No. 14. Geneva, ILO, 1969, 575-593.

Radu, E.; Lungu, C. "Récherches d'anthropologie populationelle dans la Dobroudja", in Annales Roumaines d'Anthropologie, 18 (1981), 31-39.

Reginato, E. et al. Caratteri somatici ed ematologici in un gruppo di militari di reclutamento alpino, delle provincie di Verona, Trento, Bolzano e Belluno, Atti delle Giornate Medicine delle Forze Armate, Torino, 6-7 Giugno 1961. Turin, Edizioni Minerva Medica, 1961.

Richardson, J.F.; Pincherle, G. "Heights and weights of British businessmen", in British Journal of Preventive and Social Medicine, 23 (1969), 267-270.

Riesco, J.A. "Datos antropométricos de la población laboral española", in Salud y trabajo, 19 (1979), 10-22.

Ringrose, H.; Zimmet, P. "Nutrient intakes in an urbanized Micronesian population with high diabetes prevalence", in American Journal of Clincial Nutrition, 32 (1979), 1334-1341.

Robbins, D.H.; Reynolds, H.M. Position and mobility of skeletal landmarks of the 50th percentile male in an automotive seating posture, Vehicle Research Institute Report VRI 7.1. Warendale, Pennsylvania, Society of Automotive Engineers, 15 Mar. 1975.

Roberts, D.F. "Functional anthropometry of elderly women", in Ergonomics, 3 (1960), 321-327.

Rocha, F.J. da; Salzano, F.M. "Anthropometric studies in Brazilian Cayapo Indians", in American Journal of Physical Anthropology, 36 (1972), 95-102.

Rosenbaum, S. et al. "A survey of heights and weights of adults in Great Britain, 1980", in Annals of Human Biology, 12 (1985), 115-127.

Rothhammer, F.; Spielmann, R.S. "Anthropometric variation in the Aymará: Genetic, geographic, and topographic contributions", in American Journal of Human Genetics, 24 (1972), 371-380.

8593d

Royal Air Force (RAF), Institute of Aviation Medicine (ed.). A survey of heights and weights of Royal Air Force personnel, Paper presented to the Fifth Commonwealth Defence Conference on Clothing and General Stores, Canada, 1956.

Rudan, P. et al. "Anthropometry and the biological structure of the Hvar population", in American Journal of Physical Anthropology, 70 (1986), 231-240.

Ruffie, Th. et al. "Etude biométrique du massif facial et de la denture des amérindiens Aymara et des Métis de l'altiplano Bolivien", in Bulletins et Mémoires de la Société anthropologique de Paris, Séries XI, 9 (1966), 109-116.

Russell, M. "Parent-child and sibling-sibling correlations of height and weight in a rural Guatemalean population of preschool children", in Human Biology, 48 (1976), 501-515.

Rutishauser, I.H.E.; McCay, H. "Anthropometric status and body composition in aboriginal women of the Kimberley region", in Medical Journal of Australia, Supp. 144 (1986), 8-10.

Sahbi, N. "Anthropometric measurements and work analysis related to modern technology used in the Tunisian phosphate mines", in Shahvanaz, H.; Babri, M. (eds.) Proceedings of the First International Conference on Ergonomics of Developing Countries, Lulea, Sweden, 16-17 June 1983. Lulea, CEDC, Lulea University, 1983, 96-125.

---. "Anthropométrie comparée et transfert de la technologie", in Travail Humain, 48 (1985), 47-58.

Salvendy, G. "Hand size and assembly performance", in American Institute for Industrial Engineering, Transactions, Vol. III, No. 1, 1971.

Salzano, F.M. (ed.). The ongoing evolution of Latin American populations, Springfield, Illinois, Thomas, 1971.

Sandoval Arriaga, A. "Variaciónes de algunos carácteres antropométricos en relación con la tamaño de la familia", in Anales Antropología, Universidad Nacional Autónoma, Mexico, 17 (1980), 249-268.

Santos David, J.H. "Height growth of melanodermic natives in Northeastern Luanda (Angola)", in South African Journal of Medical Sciences, 37 (1972), 49-60.

Satwanti, H. et al. "Estimation of body fat and lean body mass from anthropometric measurements in young Indian women", in Human Biology, 50 (1978), 515-527.

Schmidtke, H.; Jürgens, H.W. (eds.). Handbuch der Ergonomie, Steinebach, Luftfahrt-Verlag Walter Zuerl, 1975; Munich, Hanser, 1980.

Scott, E.C.; Bajema, C.J. "Height, weight and fertility among the participants of the third Harvard growth study", in Human Biology, 54 (1982), 501-516.

Seidler, H. "Zur Variation der Körperhöhe bei 18 jährigen Männern in Ostösterreich", in Anthropologischer Anzeiger. 44 (1986), 189-213.

Sen, R.N. "Some anthropometric studies on Indians in a tropical climate", in Proceedings of the Symposium on Environmental Physiology and Psychology in Arid Conditions, Special issue of Arid Zone Research, 24 (1964), 163-174.

---. "Some anthropometry of people of Eastern India", in Indian Anthropological Society, 12 (1977), 199-206.

Shao, Xinzhou et al. "Anthropological survey on Sibo nationality in Xinjiang Uighur autonomous region", in Acta Anthropologia Sinica, 3, 4 (1984), 349-362.

Sidhu, L.S.; Kansal, D.K. "Comparative study of body composition of Jat-Sikhs and Banias of Punjab (India)", in Zeitschrift für Morphologie und Anthropologie, 65 (1974), 276-284.

Simpson, R.E.; Bolton, C.B. An anthropometric survey of 200 RAF and RN aircrew and the application of the data to garment size rolls, TR 67125, Royal Aircraft Establishment, July 1968.

Singal, P.; Sidhu, L.S. "Age changes in skeletal diameters of two communities of Punjab (India) from 20 to 80 years", in Anthropologischer Anzeiger, 45 (1987), 71-78.

Singh, S.P. "Body morphology and anthropometric somatotypes of Rajput and Brahmin Gaddis of Dhaula Dhar Range, Himalayas", in Zeitschrift für Morphologie und Anthropologie, 72 (1981), 315-323.

Sloan, A.W.; Masali, M. "Anthropometry of Sherpa men", in Human Biology, 5 (1978), 453-458.

Slome, C. et al. "Weight, height and skinfold thickness of Zulu adults in Durban", in South African Medical Journal, 34 (1960), 505-509.

Snyder, R.G. et al. "Physical measurements of US infants, children, and teenagers", in The Highway Safety Research Institute Research Review, 7, 6 (1977), 1-19.

Soleo, L. et al. "Parametri antropometrici di un campione di popolazione femminile a lavoro in Puglia: primi risultati", in Rivista di Medicina de Lavoro ed Igiene Industriale, 4 (1980), 139-156.

Song, T.M.; Garvie, G.T. "Anthropometry, flexibility, strength, and physical measures of Canadian and Japanese olympic wrestlers", in Canadian Journal of Applied Sport Sciences, 5 (1980), 1-8.

Sporcq, J. "L'anthropologie des miliciens belges en 1963", in Bulletin d'Institut royal des Sciences naturelles de Belgique, 45 (1969), Part 32, 1-115.

Sprynar, Z. et al. "Body build, composition and functional capacity in physical education students in Algeria", in Materialy i Prace Antropologiczne, 79 (1970), 191-198.

Stefano, G.F. de; Jenkins, J.M. "Ricerche di antropologia biologica su popolazioni nicaraguensi: Nota III - Dati somatometrici", in Rivista di Antropologia, 58 (1972-73), 289-302.

Stoudt, H.W. The physical anthropology of Ceylon, Ceylon National Museums Ethnographic Series No. 2. Colombo, Colombo Museum, 1961.

---; Damon, A. "Heights and weights of White Americans", in Human Biology, 32 (1960), 331-341.

Stoudt, H.W. et al. Weight, height, and selected body dimensions of adults. United States, 1960-1962, Public Health Service Publication No. 1000, Series 11, No. 8, Washington, DC, 1965.

Strelka, F. et al. "Die Abhängigkeit des Arbeitsvermögens und der Muskelkraft der Frauen vom Lebensalter und einigen Richtwerten der somatischen Verfassung", in Acta Facultatis Rerum Naturarum Universitatis Comeniae, Anthropologica, 26-27 (1978-79), 195-213.

Strouhal, E. "Age changes of some metrical features in Nubian men", in Materialy i Prace Antropologiczne. 78 (1970), 179-190.

---. "Anthropometric and functional evidence of heterosis from Egyptian Nubia", in Human Biology, 43 (1971), 271-287.

Sukkar, M.Y. "Skinfold thickness and body fat in adult for men and women of Western Sudan", in Human Biology, 48 (1976), 315-321.

Susanne, C. "Interrelations between some social and familial factors and stature and weight of young Belgian male adults", in Human Biology, 52 (1980), 701-709.

---. Heyne, D. "Stature, poids et capacité vitale des étudiants et étudiantes de l'université libre de Bruxelles", in Bulletin de la Société royale belge, anthropologie, préhistoire, 83 (1972), 101-105.

Suzuki, H.; Kouchi, M. "Somatometric data of Chinese", in Journal of the Anthropological Society of Nippon, 94, 2 (1986), 177-181.

Takai, S.; Shimaguchi, S. "Are height and weight sufficient for the estimation of human body surface area?", in Human Biology, 58 (1986), 625-638.

Telkkä, A. "Anthropologische Untersuchung von Bewohnern der Landschaft Häme", in Annales Academiae Scientificae Fennicae, A.V. 30, 1952.

Tobias, P.V. Growth and stature in Southern African populations, Paper presented at the International Biological Programme IBP/HA Meeting in Blantyre, Malawi, 5-12 April 1971.

Tsai, Tsuli et al. "Somatological studies on the Bunun tribe in Hsin-Yi district, Nan-Tao prefecture, Taiwan, Republic of China", in Proceedings of the Eighth International Congress of Anthropological and Ethnological Sciences, 1968, Tokyo and Kyoto. Vol. I, 1970-74. Tokyo, Science Council of Japan, 1969.

Udjus, L.G. Anthropometrical changes in Norwegian men in the twentieth century. Oslo, Universitetsforlaget, 1964.

Valenzuela, C.; Avendano, A.B. "Antropometría y maduración sexual de escolares de un area de Santiago de Chile", in Boletín de la Oficina Sanitaria Panamericana, 87, 2 (1979), 113-131.

---; Rothhammer, F. "Sex dimorphism in adult stature in four Chilean populations", in Annals of Human Biology, 5 (1978), 533-538.

Valoras, V.G. "Biometric studies of army conscripts in Greece", in Human Biology, 42 (1970), 184-201.

Vargas, G.L.A. et al. "Datos antropométricos para el diseño de mobiliario escolar universitario", in Anales de Antropología, Universidad National Autónoma de México, 13 (1976), 317-326.

Vascotto, G. et al. Considerazioni sulla diversità staturale. Dati desunti da rilevamenti su militari italiani. Padua, Borghero, 1972.

Vellard, J. "Antropología física del hombre del altiplano", in Conferencia de Ciencias Antropológicas. I. Actas y Trabajos. Lima, Peru, Universidad Nacional Mayor de San Marcos de Lima, 1951.

Vidal, A. et al. "Valoración de los parámetros antropométricos en nuestra población", in Medicina Clinica, 78 (1982), 407-415.

Villiers, H. de. A study of morphological variables in urban and rural Venda male population, Paper presented at the International Biological Programme IBP/HA, Blantyre, Malawi, 5-12 April 1971.

Walker, A.R.P.; Walker, B.F. "Weight, height and triceps skinfold in South African Black, Indian and White school pupils of 18 years", in Journal of Tropical Medicine and Hygiene, 80, 6 (1977), 119-125.

Wang, Chien-Che. "Somatological studies on the Atayals tribe in Li-Shan district, Tai-Chung prefecture, Taiwan", in Anthropological Reports, 40 (1984), 1-24.

Ward, J.S. "Weights, heights and chest circumferences of English East Midlands coalminers", in Human Biology, 37 (1965), 299-311.

---; Kirk, N.S. "Anthropometry of elderly women", in Ergonomics, 10 (1967), 17-24.

---. "The relation between some anthropometric dimensions and preferred working surface heights in the kitchen", in Ergonomics, 13 (1970), 783-797.

Watson, A.W.S. "Posture and anthropometric variables in Irish males: Variations with social group and rural-urban environment", in Irish Journal of Medical Sciences, 150 (1981), 136-143.

Watson, P.E. et al. "Total body water volumes for adult males and females estimated from simple anthropometric measurements", in American Journal of Clinical Nutrition, 33 (1980), 27-39.

Weisz, J.D. Human factors engineering design standard for communication systems and related equipment, HEL Standard S-7-68. Aberdeen Proving Ground, Maryland. Army Human Engineering Laboratories, Dec. 1968.

White, R. Comparative anthropometry of the foot, Technical Report Natick/TR-83/010. Natick, Massachussetts, United States Army Natick Research and Development Laboratories, Dec. 1982.

Wiercinski, A. "Some inter- and intrapopulational comparisons in anthropometry of the inhabitants of the Western desert, Siwa Oasis, El Fayum and El Beheira", in Materialy i Prace Antroplogiczne, 78 (1970), 99-107.

Wisner, A.; Rebiffe, R. "Remarques sur la dispersion des dimensions anthropométriques et l'unicité du matériel produit en série", in Travail Humain, 26 (1963), 129-140.

Wisner, A. et al. Etude de quelques variables anthropométriques chez 8.203 demandeurs d'emploi, Report No. 44, Paris, Laboratoire de Physiologie du Travail et d'Ergonomie, Dec. 1974.

Wolanski, N.; Pyzuk, M. "Appendix I", in Studies and Human Ecology, Vol. I. Warsaw, PWN, Polish Scientific Publishers, 1973.

Wolanski, N. et al. Antropometria inzynieryjna, Kszalt i wymiary ciala a wzornictwo przemyslowe. Kzikzka i Wiedza, Warsaw, 1975, 165-225.

Wright, H.B. "Examining the individual in relation to his environment", in Bulletin of the New York Academy of Medicine, 44 (1968), 346.

Xu, Jiujin; Du, Roufu. "Study on the changes of stature of Han nationality in Beijing and Chongqing districts", in Acta Anthropologia Sinica, 4, 2 (1985), 151-159.

Yanagisawa, S. "Body proportion of the Japanese women", in Jinruigaku Zasshi (Tokyo), 69 (1961), 55-66.

Yuan, Chung-Yin. "Anthropological studies on the Yülin-li in Hainan", in Anthropological Reports, 38 (1982), 1-10.

Zentralstelle für Standardisierung des Zentralinstituts für Arbeitsmedizin der DDR: TGL 22 315 Blatt 1 - Arbeitshygiene, Arbeitsplatzmasse, Körpermasse. Zitiert nach: Quaas, M.; Renker, U. (eds.). Arbeitshygiene. Berlin, Volk und Gesundheit, 1976.

8593d

Zolotareva, I.M.   "The Khalkha Mongols and the race types of Northern Asia", in Proceedings of the Eighth International Congress of Anthropological and Ethnological Sciences, 1968, Tokyo and Kyoto.   Vol. I, 177–179.   Tokyo, Science Council of Japan, 1969.